HERALDRY IN THE CATHOLIC CHURCH

PAX
TIBI
MARCE

EVANGE
LISTA
MEUS

Immediately following the election of Cardinal Albino Luciani to the papacy, the author designed the coat of arms for the new Pontiff who had taken the name John Paul I in memory of his two predecessors. The Pope communicated his wishes to the author on the day following the election and on August 28, 1978, two designs were submitted to His Holiness. The Pope adopted the traditional design for general use.

The arms of Pope John Paul I, Albino Luciani, b. October 17, 1912, cons. bishop December 27, 1958, Patriarch of Venice December 15, 1969 and created a cardinal on March 5, 1973. He was elected to the papacy on August 26, 1978.

His Holiness died on the morning of September 29, 1978 after a reign of only 33 days.

HERALDRY IN THE CATHOLIC CHURCH
ITS ORIGIN, CUSTOMS AND LAWS

Bruno Bernard Heim

VAN DUREN
GERRARDS CROSS 1978
and
HUMANITIES PRESS, NEW JERSEY

First published in October 1978 in the United Kingdom by Van Duren Contract Publications Limited of Gerrards Cross, Buckinghamshire, SL9 7AE, England.

CIP Data : United Kingdom
Heim, Bruno Bernard
Heraldry in the Catholic Church.
 1. Heraldry, Sacred
 I. Title
 926.6   CR1101

CR
1101
H44
1978

ISBN 0-905715-05-5

United States of America :

Humanities Press Inc., New Jersey.
ISBN 0-391-00873-0
Library of Congress Number 78-569 36

This book was set by Keith Lawrence of Watford, Hertfordshire, printed and bound by A. Wheaton & Co. Ltd. of Exeter, Devon. Colour separations by Dolphin Reproduction, Aylesbury, Buckinghamshire.

The *heraldic fantasia* on the book jacket was specially designed by the author for this publication.

CONTENTS

CONTENTS

(Continued)

COLOUR PLATES

The heraldic fantasia on the front and back of the jacket has also been inserted in the book on two seperate plates.

ACKNOWLEDGEMENTS

The preparation of a book such as this would not have been possible without the collaboration of many hands, and due respects must properly be paid to some of those people and organisations who gave unstintingly of their help. Firstly, thanks are tendered to Dr John Tanner, whose scholarly assistance with the text was of incalculable value. It is no exaggeration to record that but for his learning and devoted labours, in the midst of a busy public life, this volume would not yet be ready to lay before the public.

Similarly, the Reverend Richard Frost, Mr Michael McCarthy, Cecil R. Humphery-Smith and Professor Geza Grosschmid, all contributed from the store of their linguistic and heraldic knowledge, and the book owes much to all three, as it does to the unrivalled resources of The College of Arms and the Heraldry Society.

Heraldic seals are of outstanding significance in the study of ecclesiastical heraldry and to Rudolf Niedballa, the contemporary master of engraving, a particular debt is owed. He has executed Pope John's and Pope Paul's and the many bishop's seals featured in this book and thereby enriched and illuminated an entire field in a style uniquely his own. The author has to thank him for 25 years of enjoyable collaboration and mutual inspiration.

Finally, the preparation of this volume for the press was lifted from the realm of labour to that of undiluted pleasure by the co-operation of my publishers, Dr Peter Bander and Mr Leslie Hayward, who devised the layout and melded text and illustrations together in a fashion beyond criticism. To these, and to all those friends who gave advice and encouragement, the author's warmest and most sincere thanks are tendered.

Bruno B. Heim.

Bruno Bernard Heim

HERALDRY IN THE CATHOLIC CHURCH
ITS ORIGIN, CUSTOMS AND LAWS

CHAPTER ONE

I

THE ORIGINS AND DEVELOPMENT
OF HERALDRY

Thanks to its brilliant colours, its power of suggestion and the rich store of symbols it has accumulated, the noble art of heraldry has been a source of deep and mysterious enchantment for many people down the ages. Nonetheless, few are truly familiar with its rules, its characteristic style and its peculiar language, because possession of this knowledge presupposes years of study and intelligent observation.

Hence heraldry remains an esoteric subject as far as the general public is concerned. Moreover, scholars in the discipline were in early times, too frequently unconcerned to popularize their science, and in spite of the abundance of armoiral devices that attract general attention too much heraldic literature contains too many unjustified generalisations and unfounded statements.

Armorial bearings first made their appearance among medieval warriors as personal, and later family, signs of identification. From the beginning of the Twelfth Century they displayed personal signs on their armour – in particular on the shield and the helmet. The earliest true heraldic arms would appear to be those of Geoffrey V, Count of Anjou, known as Plantagenet. They date from 1127 A.D.

From the several theories on the origin of armorial bearings it seems reasonable to single out that which is linked to the development of the knight's helmet. The contemporary method of warfare required a knight to wear a helmet and carry a shield to counter his enemy's weapons, and the former completely enclosed the head, with only a narrow slit to see through and a few holes for air, thus effectively concealing the wearer's identity.

Medieval helms and crests of the Dukes of Norfolk.

The practical necessity of being recognized by comrades-in-arms, and the natural human desire to possess magnificently decorated armour, (not exclusively worn on military expeditions, but in tournaments as well) induced the knights to mark their shields and helmets with brightly coloured devices which were visible from afar. These distinctive signs are called armorial bearings.

At the same time as embellishing the knight's armour in a splendid fashion, these devices had other and obvious advantages and their use spread rapidly through the greater part of Europe. Before long one could see arms engraved on seals, decorating the exteriors of castles and other dwellings, and on many household objects; they were embroidered on the caparisons of horses and sculptured on funeral monuments.

Armorial devices were painted on the shields and appeared in full-relief on the helm. The crest was often a modelled reproduction of a charge painted on the shield. The helm was nearly always draped with a covering or mantling, usually in the same tinctures or colours as the shield. There was a good reason for this mantling in that it served to shade the metal helm from the direct rays of the sun.

In this classical "living" period of heraldry the achievement quite simply consisted of the decorated shield, the crested helmet and the mantling.

Such was the original composition of the knight's achievement in the Middle Ages. There was nothing to indicate the rank of the person who bore the arms, and no special marks to distinguish dukes from counts, or barons from knights. Sometimes sovereigns (emperors and kings) wore a crown on their helmet in allusion to their dignity. We should note in passing that wreaths and coronets, which were often used to conceal the joint between the helmet and the crest, had no more than decorative value.

The merit of having given birth to the art and practice of heraldry was in past years attributed to the crusades and tournaments, but in fact they were merely the occasions which served to increase the use of armorial bearings, and, as can be readily understood, contributed to their widespread popularity and indispensability.

The increasing use of firearms from the Fourteenth Century onwards meant that armour no longer provided

Equestrian seal of Amadaeus V, Count of Savoy, c.1307.

sufficient protection for the warrior. Its sheer weight became a hindrance to mobility, now increasingly important. New techniques in armaments had dictated the development of armour, and now ensured its obsolescence towards the end of the Fifteenth Century. By this time, however, armorial bearings had well-established secondary uses, which now became their principal functions and have remained so to the present day.

The custom of using emblems for military, legal, domestic or decorative purposes is as ancient as any civilization, even primitive, and existed long before armorial bearings came into being. It is an inalienable right for everybody to have a name and to possess personal signs by which he may be recognized. In antiquity, such signs were already in evidence among eastern and western peoples; they were also known among the aboriginal Americans.

The Greeks and Romans, particularly, made frequent use of emblems of war, and were fond of putting symbols on their rings and coinage. They also put marks of ownership on tools and vases. Similar customs can be traced very early on among the Japanese, Huns, Goths, Lombards, Angles, Saxons, Franks, Danes, Normans, Moors, Saracens and many other peoples. While not heraldry proper these marks served partly the same basic original purpose – ease of identification.

Heraldry can be divided into three periods from the point of view of its historical evolution :

1. *Heraldry of warfare* :
       (Twelfth and Thirteenth Centuries)
2. *Tournament heraldry* :
       (Fourteenth and Fifteenth Centuries)
3. *Ornamental heraldry* :
       (from Sixteenth Century onwards)

The first two periods are those in which heraldry really lived, since the coats of arms were actually worn and used for their original purposes. With the third period heraldry became a proud memory of a glorious past, but also a distinguished and popular art that had evolved new uses and a life of its own.

From the particular point of view of heraldry as an

Pharaonic standards of Egyptian provinces. Roman, Saracen and Egyptian symbols.

11

Egyptian (top left) and Japanese family symbols.

Unicorn: the expression of ferocity typifies fourteenth century usage.

art form, it can be divided according to the various styles of decorative art.

Roughly speaking, classical heraldry corresponds with the Gothic period in art. After this, the military necessity to use a shield and helmet having vanished, one can witness, with the advent of the Renaissance, Baroque and Rococo periods, an almost universal decline of the original and proper style of heraldic art.

Throughout these periods one can find splendid works of art, particularly in the field of sculpture, but one has to recognize that these styles were over-rich and lavish in ornament and had a regrettable effect on heraldic design, particularly on the Continent.

In more recent decades there has been a new blossoming of the art, and development of better taste in heraldry. This trend is promoted in many countries through specialist societies and encourages a return to those simpler forms which are not only closer to the original spirit and ethos of medieval heraldry but accord better with the taste of our time.

Before studying the question of heraldic law it is desirable to glance at the basic principles which govern the art of heraldry.

The supreme law of heraldic design is visibility, arising from the need to see clearly the charges on the shield and helmet in order to recognize their bearer even from a distance and in the heat of battle. This was, as earlier explained, the "raison d'être" of heraldic ornaments.

As far as the shield is concerned, heraldic design is restricted to two dimensions. It cannot tolerate, one might say, either perspective or shading. Its divisions are geometric. In the representation of any kind of heraldic charges all unnecessary details are suppressed and absolute realism is avoided. Heraldic art gives pride of place to the characteristics and purity of outline. The main features of figures are exaggerated to such a degree that they often become a kind of caricature. A certain constancy of type is also demanded and animals for example, by the time of Bartolus de Saxoferrato (1350), were supposed to appear at their fiercest and most aggressive.

As a general rule, the charges should occupy the whole shield, harmoniously, as if suspended within it, without touching the edges at any point. Clarity, as has been already said, is the essential quality of heraldic art.

The result is a particular form of stylization which does not rule out freedom of expression, liveliness of line or elegance. In order to make the best use of this freedom, the artist needs a thorough knowledge and wide experience of heraldry, which, of necessity, takes a long time to acquire. It is ease in handling this freedom of creation that reveals the erudition and mastery of an artist-herald.

In order to make their shields more easily recognizable, the medieval knights painted them in strongly contrasting colours. This was the origin of the innumerable partitions and ordinaries which can be found in every handbook of heraldry.

Apart from these near-geometrical signs they used heraldic charges including human figures, members of the body, animals, parts of animals, monsters, plants, leaves, flowers, fruit, stars, religious symbols, tools, marks of trade or profession, and many other devices.

The infinite number of heraldic charges, together with the possibility of changing their position on the shield and different colouring by heraldic tinctures (gules – red; azure – blue; vert – green; sable – black) and metals (or – gold, yellow; argent – silver, white) offer an immense variety of differentiation.

There has never existed a mysterious or runic symbolism special to heraldry, as some authors maintain. The pretended "heraldic symbolism" was simply a reflection of popular belief, and currently held notions. The symbolic meanings of animals like the lion, the eagle and the dove are well known to everybody. Similarly with stars, hearts, crosses, flowers and objects like tools; their symbolism is intelligible to all.

Why someone chose a particular colour or emblem might be, and remain, obscure for ever. The reason for a choice could lie in a feat of arms, an important event or some incident now forgotten and untraceable. It could also have resided in some personal quality of the bearer, or be a matter of pure whim or imagination. For the most part the reasons for a choice are unknown to us, unless it be a matter of canting arms – and they are not all that numerous – where there is some allusion to a person's name or occupation or some well known historical event.

Heraldry has not only got its own artistic forms, it possesses, in addition, a very particular technical

The arms of the Princes of Schwarzenberg. That depicted is of Prince Karl, who as a Bailiff of Honour and Devotion in the Order of Malta uses the arms of the Order in chief; this usage is known as the chief of religion.

The arms of the American industrialist Frank Schneider. The quarterings show the canting arms (Schneider = tailor) and symbols of his business interests.

13

The arms of the Swedish Counts Bielke (above) and the Grand Dukes of Luxembourg. Both arms date from the Middle Ages.

language all of its own. The remarkable quality of this language is its conciseness. Its style is elegant but austere. Blazoning should be brief, without any possible ambiguity and of a perfect technical exactness. In this respect the French Heralds were the masterminds; they were the first to perfect blazoning of the most difficult arms, without omitting anything useful or adding a superfluous word. No one has ever surpassed them at this. English blazoning, borrowing its vocabulary largely from the French, also established itself early on, but the Germans had to wait for one Maximilian Gritzner, who in 1889 finally established a definitive terminology, having the indispensable precision needed. The Italian system of blazoning is likewise but recently established.

As had been said before, at the outset experts in heraldry were very few and they originally handed on their knowledge by word of mouth. With the widespread use of printing came the appearance of a specialist literature which grew copiously, and included in the nigh-endless list of authors are such prominent names as :

Conrad of Mure, Bartolus of Saxoferrato, Bishops John Trevor of St. Asaph and Bernard du Rosier of Toulouse, Canon Nicholas Upton, Leigh, Boswell, Wyrley, Chasseneux, Vulson de la Colombière, Hoeping, Father Menestrier S. J., Le Laboureur, Palliot, Spener, Gatterer, Berry, Boutell, Planché, Piferrer, Crollalanza, Hauptmann, Ströhl, Clark, Gevaert, Woodward, Bouly de Lesdain, Anthony Wagner, Galbreath, and Fox-Davies.

The great attention paid by a vast public to heraldic questions, in spite of the disappearance of living heraldry in the original concept of that phrase, cannot be accounted for simply by an interest in historical studies. If arms have disappeared as distinguishing marks on armour, this has in no way lessened their representational worth and their continued living popularity.

Beginning with the Twelfth Century, ladies of the nobility, and from the Thirteenth Century other non-combatants like clerics, members of the middle-classes and peasants, have followed the proud custom of the knights and adopted armorial bearings. In the same way corporations (public authorities and departments) and ecclesiastical bodies (bishoprics, abbeys and chapters, for example) adopted them early on to stamp and seal documents of an official nature.

Their use being no longer limited to war and tournaments, arms had become personal identification signs which, applied to objects, indicated ownership. They further became symbols of sovereignty, jurisdiction, protection, territorial claims, and were universally considered as marks of honour. It goes without saying, then, that they have acquired universal usefulness and attractiveness.

One of the principal and most extensive uses of arms still remains to be considered. That is their use on seals. There were few who could write in the Middle Ages, and the use of seals provided the chief means of assuring the legal validity and authenticity of all contracts and written documents.

Even to-day, the seal which corroborates a signature has the same purpose, and perhaps no Government in the world is without its seal of State. Small wonder that even in the old democracies like Switzerland, as much as in America, the study of heraldry flourishes with remarkable vigour to this day, for the origins and manifold uses of coats of arms have made them full of symbolic significance and of international application.

From being a distinctive mark of personal identification in battle, the coat of arms has become a sign of that personal code which all men wish to defend. The arms represent, so to speak, a programme of life for one who bears them. They invite him to be faithful to himself and to his principles. They become like names, something which is inherited, and which speaks of the honour and dishonour, the success and ruin of a family through the generations. They pass from people to the land and from the land back to the people. They are adopted as the emblems of towns and communities, and as symbols of the sovereignty of nations. They serve this serious function to-day even in the U.S.S.R. where, for the most part, the arms of the republics are those of the hammer and sickle and star. In 1930 many districts and municipalities still bore images and symbols of Saints in their seals. Later they have been "cleansed" from their historical "holy" devices – but only to be replaced by what is still undeniably heraldry.

1270

Early portrait seals from Finland.

1288

15

The arms of Anti-Pope Benedict XIII.

(above and right)
Two Finnish portrait seals of 1398 and 1423 showing the introduction of the shield.

HERALDIC LAW

Seals imprinting symbols, effigies and armorial bearings achieved status as first order legal instruments and themselves became objects of law. Considering the frequency of their use and authority, one understands easily that they provoked widespread covetousness. They became the object of manifold legal transactions which were first regulated by custom and, subsequently, by special legislation.

Neither the heralds of old, nor the jurists who were thus involved, studied the basis of heraldic law, and very often they do not even remark on it. It is only incidentally that early heraldic treatises make mention of legal considerations. The formative authors and their major works are worthy of passing reference.

The only medieval jurist to attempt the formulation of a few rules of heraldic law, based on Roman Law, was the distinguished commentator Bartolus of Saxoferrato (d. 1357) in a little heraldic treatise published posthumously. This is one of the first pamphlets on heraldry, brief and containing but little juridical material. The fame of the author nonetheless gave the work a great success, and it was often noted by later scholars, notably by Felix Hemmerlin, a canon of Zurich, in his treatise *De Nobilitate et Rusticitate* (1444); by Peter of Andlaw in his script *De Imperio Romano Germanico* (1460); and by numerous Fifteenth Century authors of treatises on blazoning.

Bernard du Rosier, Archbishop of Toulouse (d. 1475) also belongs to the Bartolian school, and before his elevation to the episcopate in 1437 he composed a manuscript on heraldry in which he improves on the master, adding new material. In fact he considerably developed the doctrine of the illustrious Italian jurist on the attributes or badges of rank, bringing it into line with the usages which had come into force in the meantime, especially with regard to the insignia of the ecclesiastical hierarchy.

Bartelemy de Chasseneux added further ideas in his *Catalogus Gloriae Mundi* (1546).

In the Sixteenth Century Scohier, in his *Etat et Comportement des Armes* (1629), deals especially with cadency. Theodore Hoeping, on the other hand, (*De Insignium et Armorum Prisco et Novo Jure, 1642*), remains a disciple of Bartolus and still follows Roman Law. He solves questions of heraldic law according to the norms of the *Corpus Juris* on senatorial dignity and the *Jus Imaginum*.

In 1668 Jean-Baptiste Christyn, baron of Meerbeek, and Chancellor of Brabant, published his *Jurisprudentia Heroica* and under the guise of a commentary on the edict of the Archduke Albert and the Archduchess Isabella of 14th December, 1616, he offered for the first time a synthesis of the heraldic law of the Catholic Netherlands.

The *Dissertatio de Insignibus Eorumque Jure* (1672) by Sebastian Fesch of Basle, is no more than an abridgement of Hoeping.

More recently, Otto Titan von Hefner, published a series of theses in six chapters, albeit incomplete, on heraldic law in his book *Altbayrische Heraldik* (1863).

Felix Hauptmann has written more extensively in his work *Das Wappenrecht* (1896), which was the accepted authority for a long time. His fundamental notion of the right to bear arms being restricted to privileged classes is, however, built on false premises and is not borne out by the facts. To-day it has been completely abandoned. The right to bear arms has become increasingly general and even in countries which still have a heraldic jurisdiction, like Great Britain, Coats of Arms are granted to all suitable supplicants.

In 1924 Nisot published his *Le Droit des Armoiries*. The value of this work is also diminished by his interpretation of the right to bear arms, which is not supported by the practice of the Middle Ages, but falsely deduced from more recent legislation in certain countries regarding nobiliary matters.

Finally, there are the works of Walter Freier: *Wappenkunde und Wappenrecht* (1924) and Lucien Fourez: *Le Droit Héraldique des Pays-Bas Catholiques* (1932) which was based on Christyn, and lastly the interesting work of Remi Mathieu: *Le Système*

The arms of Pope Gregory XII and Anti-Pope Benedict XIII, taken from 'Das Concilium' by Ulrich von Richenthal of 1413.

17

Two versions of the arms of the ancient baronial families of Mowbray and Segrave illustrating the wide divergence of style permissible, each being correct. The arms, consisting of one charge, typify the purity of medieval heraldry.

Héraldique Français (1946) which is solidly based on historical facts.

What, then, are the origins of heraldic law? We have seen that knights, for practical and military reasons, began to decorate their armour with distinctive signs in order to make themselves recognisable. This is the obvious reason for the first of the rules of armorial bearings, that of exclusiveness. In virtue of this rule, it was forbidden to assume, knowingly and without permission, the heraldic emblems adopted by another. Considering the almost unlimited possibilities of choice available when adopting armorial bearings, it would have been inexcusable to have violated the rights of others. If armorial bearings were not the exclusive property of an individual, a family or corporation, they would have lost their distinctive value.

Originally charges and colours were a matter of free choice. It often happened that certain noblemen changed their arms several times, at will.

The scions of a knight frequently adopted the same profession of arms, and by preference adopted the emblems that their father had worn and perhaps made famous, and thus a coat of arms very quickly became hereditary. Through arms one showed that one belonged to a certain lineage, and it was natural that abuses in this matter led to understandable quarrels.

At times armorial bearings passed from a family to a fief, and the succeeding feudatories adopted them on acquiring the lands. Here we have a third manner of appropriation, differing from free choice and inheritance.

Who had the publicly recognized and guaranteed right to bear arms? At the outset there was no doubt about it – those who needed arms as distinguishing marks on their armour – warriors or knights. The right to bear arms went hand in hand with the profession of a knight, which was entered into, above all but not solely, through birth and by dubbing.

In the course of time newcomers appeared who aspired to advantages and consideration; they served under arms and rose to positions formerly occupied by the nobility.

By the middle of the Thirteenth Century some members of the middle classes assumed arms, in imitation of the nobility, and a century later peasant coats of arms can be found.

It was only with the disappearance of living heraldry that certain legal theorists tried to propagate the idea (which later even inspired legislation in some countries) that the right to bear arms was exclusively reserved to the nobility, and such burghers as had attained the privilege through a concession of the sovereign.

Yet it is the birthright of any human being to bear names and signs which distinguish him from another person. This right is limited by the corresponding right of the others, and it is clearly inadmissible for someone to appropriate the emblems of rank, office, or dignity to which he is not entitled.

Under pressure of financial necessity, some monarchs arrogated to themselves the right to authorize the bearing of arms, requiring that everyone registered his arms for approval and then paid a tax on them.

Thus it came about that since the middle of the Fifteenth Century the free composition of armory was repeatedly forbidden, and has remained so in many countries until to-day, although in some States political or social upheaval has profoundly changed the outlook.

In our times the initial freedom to compose one's own armorial bearings at will is almost universally recognized, save in those countries where the Crown or State reserves to itself the right of control.

Where sovereigns have reserved to themselves the right to confer armorial bearings, this right is exercised either directly or by granting the power to certain dignitaries, like the Counts Palatine in the Holy Roman Empire and the former Kings of Arms in France, or to the College of Arms and Lyon Court in the United Kingdom.

The Bartolian school, while according to every man the right freely to adopt arms, attributes more honour to arms granted by a prince.

Arms were granted either *in forma meliori* by letters patent, or *in forma communi* by simple letters of arms.

Ennoblement always brings with it the bearing of a coat of arms. A simple grant of arms, on the contrary, does not necessarily confer nobility, although some jurisdictions state in their patents that the recipients are thus of the "noblesse". Therefore, heraldic law must be carefully distinguished from true nobiliary law.

Heraldic law is based on the one hand on related customs, and on the other hand on special legislation. Both private and public law are involved. The privilege

The official arms of Garter King of Arms.

19

Mgr. Callori di Vignale, major-domo of Pope Pius XII, impaled his family arms with the arms of the Pope.

Mgr. Capovilla was private secretary to Pope John XXIII. After the Pope's death he became an archbishop and adopted Pope John's coat of arms. To mark a difference he omitted one of the two fleurs-de-lis.

of bearing arms would be a question of public law, whereas the right to bear a specific coat of arms would depend on private law.

The right to bear arms, *"la capacité heraldique"*, is a general right, not a privilege, and belongs to any man excepting one from whom the right may have been withdrawn by the public authority as a result of certain crimes. This natural law to use signs or symbols as a kind of "moral portrait" would not exclude governmental control and protection.

Those entitled to bear arms are classed quite simply as individuals, families and corporations. During the thirteenth and fourteenth centuries the custom of using armorial bearings passed slowly to individuals and societies of all social classes.

The rules governing the use of heraldic marks of dignity which are officially recognised are a matter of public law. In the case of secular heraldry this applies, for example, to the various crowns indicating ranks of nobility, according to the usages spread in the seventeenth century; for ecclesiastical heraldry, to the various hierarchical insignia of the clergy. The characteristic meaning of the latter, and their application in heraldry, will form the principal object of this study.

The second part of heraldic law concerns the ownership of a specific achievement. The law regards the ideal and not the material object; that is to say, what is represented by the specific heraldic emblems and tinctures, rather than the achievement itself. The right to a specific achievement is the right to bear this particular coat of arms. In principle, this right is exclusive, but the exercise of it in certain countries has included a certain freedom of disposal which even allowed the transfer and sale of a coat of arms.

In principle, as previously made plain, everyone is allowed the right to bear arms; nevertheless, there are procedures which govern the acquisition and loss of a specific and personal achievement. The absolute freedom of choice is limited by rights acquired by third parties or legislation.

As we have seen, the first method of acquiring an achievement was the spontaneous adoption of certain emblems and colours. To a large extent this free adoption was replaced by the granting of a specific coat of arms by the sovereign.

The most frequent way in which the secondary acquisition of arms takes place is through inheritance, by right of birth. Arms are then subject to the common and statutory laws which govern the legal consequences of legitimate and illegitimate descent, or from birth resulting out of a morganatic marriage or a misalliance. The effects of legitimitisation, whether by subsequent marriage of the parents or by the legal recognition of the father, or by an act of the sovereign, depends on the legislation in force in a particular country.

Marriage is another secondary method of acquisition of armorial bearings. Here again, a distinction must be drawn between a marriage where there is an equality of birth, and the morganatic union or misalliance. A great deal more might be said on the question of the acquisition of coats of arms; also their loss through renunciation, divorce, certain omissions, and crimes. These developments can be ignored for the purpose of this study, for the heraldic law of the Church deals only with the marks of dignity of clerics and ignores their heraldic shields.

Besides his own arms someone may, in certain circumstances, possess or use arms belonging to others, whether individuals, communities or institutions. Their acquisition may come about in several ways, of which we shall mention only those having a bearing on ecclesiastical arms. Many clerics belong to religious orders or congregations in which it is customary, if they attain office therein, for them to marshal both personal and corporate arms together.

For example, the Sovereign Military Order of St. John of Jerusalem (the Order of Malta) extends to its professed members of high rank, and to those who have the bailiff's cross of honour and devotion, the right to incorporate the arms of the Sovereign Order in chief on their personal shields. This is known as a Chief of Religion. In a similar way the members – and especially the superiors – of the Dominican Order have the custom of marshalling their personal arms with those of the Order and placing the whole shield on a cross fleur-de-lys.

As a sign of office many prelates and bishops marshal their personal arms with those of their diocese, territories, monasteries or chapters. This custom is rare in Italy and almost non-existent in France, but common in many

An example of arms acquired through marriage. Queen Elizabeth the Queen Mother impales her family arms, Bowes Lyon, with the royal arms.

The arms of the Dominican Father Henry de Riedmatten are placed on a cross fleurette which is also a symbol of the Dominican Order.

21

The seal of the Republic of Malagasy.

The embossed eagles of the German Empire (until 1918) and the Federal Republic (since 1948) (Engraved by R. Niedballa).

other countries, including the USA, Austria, Germany and Switzerland.

In the same way, augmentations granted by the sovereign as a sign of favour can be added to existing arms, thus allowing certain subjects to bear charges of honour including, occasionally, those taken from the sovereign's own achievement.

Finally, there are commemorative arms recalling historical events. In this way the families of Popes have added the Church's arms to their own: the basilical pavilion, (a very special form of umbrella), with the papal keys.

To-day there are few countries which possess a written heraldic law. The character of the state, needless to say, is of prime importance in this respect. Naturally enough, a monarchy will normally pay more attention to heraldic law than a republic. In a monarchy the granting, bearing, transmission and registration of arms will at least be regulated. Other states customarily allow total freedom as far as usage is concerned. Some states recognise and protect armorial bearings; others forbid or abolish them, establishing legal penalties for delinquents. This has happened notably during the course of political upheavals, especially in France at the time of the Revolution. The Revolutionary Law of June 15th, 1790, followed by the Decrees of September 27th, October 16th, 1791, and August 1st, 1793, threatened the severest of penalties for those who persisted in using armorial bearings. In March 1808, however, Napoleon brought them back into favour by the creation of a new system of heraldry and nobility.

Democratic countries are today generally disinterested in the customs with which we are concerned, and tend to allow their citizens total freedom in this respect. Having no legal status, personal arms are not public emblems of rank or office and only by accident do they figure in legal procedings, when it is more a matter of violating other rights, such as in a case of fraud related to genealogical or heraldic research.

III

THE USE OF ARMS IN THE CHURCH

We might well ask how and why did armorial bearings come to be used by the Church, seeing that they were first and foremost military in origin and purpose? The profession of a fighting man has always been, and still is, strictly forbidden for clerics (Canons 138 and 141 (Codex Juris Canonici). Indeed, from the birth to the height of the heraldic age, the clerics were forbidden to carry arms under threat of excommunication and it was considered a scandal if they did.

Even if they belonged to a knightly family clerics were not permitted to use arms in the manner of secular knights, and if they ignored the prohibition they incurred public opprobrium.

We have seen that at the beginning of heraldry arms were inseparably connected with war and tournaments. If the clergy were forbidden to take part in warlike exploits, they were even more strongly forbidden to take part in tournaments. These often bloody and murderous events were always condemned by the Church under pain of excommunication. They were even, with little success, forbidden for laymen.

At first the princes of the Church hesitated to make use of armorial bearings. It was exceptional to find Guillaume de Joinville, Bishop of Langres (1209-1215), making use of the arms of his territory without the addition of any ecclesiastical symbols. The study of seals reveals that, with few exceptions, it was not until the middle of the thirteenth century that armorial bearings were widely used in the Church, well over a century after their origin among the nobility. At that time, arms, although still used for their original purposes, were widely employed as personal marks and adornments.

It was primarily because of their usefulness as seal emblems that Coats of Arms became popular in the Church, it being realised promptly that armorial devices were ideal for such a purpose, having all the desirable qualities.

At first, however, there was a marked hesitation to attribute armorial bearings to clerics. In the Zürich Roll

The battle-standard of the Bishop of Basle, taken from the Zurich Wappenrolle.

The arms of two abbots who combined ecclesiastical and temporal marks of dignity: helmet, sword, mitre and crozier.

Dominus Iohannes Epifcopus Norvvicenfis.

The arms of the Bishop of Norwich as recorded for the Council of Constance. The present-day Anglican See retains the three mitres in its arms.

Dominus Thomas Polcan de, canus. Et Prothonotarius Re, gis Anglie.

Dominus

From the same archives come the arms of Thomas Polcan; not being a bishop, the protonotary's arms should not be adorned with mitre and crozier.

of Arms, (*Zürcher Wappenrolle,*) dating from 1240, there are twenty-seven prelates' arms; these are not painted as usual on shields, but on banners. Princes of the Church could not take part in military expeditions personally, or arm themselves with shields and helmets. Nonetheless, they were bound to supply the sovereign with their feudal contingent, who needed to be visually identifiable.

Ladies did not go to war either. Yet by the second half of the twelfth century there were seals in use which proved that noblewomen adopted with pride, as personal emblems, the shield of arms belonging to their fathers or husbands.

A few years after the composition of the Zürich Roll of Arms, the *Codex Seffken,* known as the *"Wappenbuch von den Ersten,"* depicts episcopal arms with helms and shields.

The use of the coat of arms was so wide-spread in secular society at that time that it was impossible to take exception at seeing clergy adopt it in their turn, and the adoption of armorial bearings very quickly became general among the clergy. The Bishops Miles de Nanteuil (1222), Robert de Cressonsart (1240) and Guillaume de Gretz (1261) used the arms of the bishopric of Beauvais. Guy de Rochefort, Bishop of Langres in 1263, was the first Bishop to adorn his seal with a shield bearing the arms of his family. In the case of other Bishops, some waited until the Fourteenth Century before making use of armorial seals; for example, the Bishops of Coire in Switzerland.

Family arms appear earlier on the seals of clergy of lower rank. Rémi Mathieu mentions Nicholas, Archdeacon of Valenciennes in 1236 and Hunon de la Fosse, Canon of Saint Quentin in 1239, as having made use of family arms before the middle of the Thirteenth Century. We can add Rudolph de Frobourg, Provost of Zofingue, who, in 1245, used the arms of the Counts of Frobourg as a seal.

Although heraldry received a ready reception throughout the hierarchy of the Church, and its use was frequent and manifold in all forms of ecclesiastical art, and despite the immense amount of heraldic literature produced, we possess but a few works which are devoted entirely to ecclesiastical heraldry. More than one hundred years ago Mgr. Barbier de Montault published an essay on the heraldic legislation of the Church, but it is far from

The tomb of Pope Boniface VIII, r. 1294-1303, with five shields of his arms. The double-crowned tiara dates from his pontificate and he was probably the first Pope to use inherited arms.

complete. There is no such thing as a complete synthesis of the Church's heraldic laws but, because ecclesiastical arms are to be found in abundance, there are many chapters in heraldry manuals which are devoted to ecclesiastical seals in a summary way, and substantial articles can be found in periodicals, dictionaries and encyclopaedias.

We can mention John Woodward and Donald Lindsay Galbreath as authors of fundamental and important works. The latter eminent author has rendered an enormous service to the science of ecclesiastical heraldry, especially through his work *Papal Heraldry,* (1930, re-edited 1972, London, Heraldry today).

Among other authors who have contributed to the knowledge of ecclesiastical heraldic usage we might name: Mgr. Albert Battandier, the Count of Saint-Saud, H. G. Ströhl, Henri Dubrulle, Baron du Roure de Paulin, Count Pasini Frassoni, Max Prinet, Eugène Harot, André Cosson and F. Th. Dubois.

Arms of the Bishop of Salisbury from 'Das Concilium'. He is erroneously described as 'a powerful Archbishop who died here...'

The seals of the Bishop and Diocese of Reykjavik.

All the modern seals on this and ensuing pages were designed by the author and engraved by Rudolf Niedballa in Germany.

CHAPTER TWO

I

THE USE OF ARMORIAL BEARINGS IN ECCLESIASTICAL SEALS

Coats of Arms entered the Church by way of the seal. Some long time before the birth of armory, quite apart from the Lords and their functionaries, officials of the Church had the right to seals, that is to say, they were empowered to authenticate documents and contracts, sealing them with their signets. Apart from this secular use of seals by the clergy, the Code of Canon Law required the use of seals, and still does. Nevertheless, the wax seal is often less practical than the embossing press, or the rubber-stamp, and is often replaced by them. Stamps serve the same purpose, in part, as seals, and they are included in the meaning of *sigillum,* which is repeated so often in the Code of Canon Law.

1

THE REGULATIONS OF THE CODE OF CANON LAW RELATIVE TO THE USE OF SEALS:

It is not our intention to enumerate here all the regulations of the Church concerning the use of seals and stamps. We shall mention only the canons of the Code which prescribe their use, to show that they still have a current importance.

The following are the relevant Canons :

1) Canon 381, § 2, supposes the existence of Curial seals, dealing as it does with archives, and the secret episcopal archives, for, when an episcopal see is vacant, the archives should be sealed up.

2) The Curial Seals are mentioned three times in Canon 382. Their importance and inviolability appear in it clearly. Paragraph two of this canon provides that on the arrival of a new Bishop in a diocese the vicar capitular, should the seals have been broken by him and the cabinet of secret

archives opened, must give without delay an account of the reasons leading to such action.

3) Canon 450, § 1, orders that the deans be provided with a special seal, for the function of the dean is a public charge and his testimony is proof in the domain of Canon Law, and often in that of secular jurisdiction.

4) Canon 470, § 4, prescribes a parochial seal. The parish priest is also a public official, and as such has the right and duty to possess a seal which he uses on birth, confirmation, marriage and death certificates, and which he needs for his official correspondence.

5) Canon 545, § 1, orders the sealing of testimonials concerning aspirants to the religious life.

6) According to Canon 1287, § 1, relics must be enclosed in boxes or capsules, sealed in such a way that they may not be taken out without breaking the seal. The right to authenticate relics is granted formally by Canon 1283 to Cardinals and prelates who have episcopal jurisdiction, (*Ordinarii locorum*). This seal which protects relics is explicitly mentioned in the document which declares their authenticity. The dimensions of this seal are often small and only allow room for the shield and emblems of rank.

7) Canonical procedure requires the affixing of many seals. Canon 1643, § 1, insists that each page of the records be numbered, signed and sealed.

8) If anyone is summoned to appear before an ecclesiastical court, the summons must be signed and sealed. (Canon 1715, § 2).

9) Canon 2041, § 2, gives grave instructions on the subject of the use of seals in proceedings of beatification and canonization. Here it is a question of the sealing of the records between sessions, and of the formal verification of the integrity of the seals at the opening of every new session. If ever these seals are found to be broken, the judge (here we are dealing with diocesan proceedings) is obliged to inform the Holy See.

10) Canon 2055, still on the same subject, lays down that the *Transumptum* (that is to say, the manuscript copy of the proceedings) must be signed and sealed as a proof of its authenticity, by the notary, judge and promoter.

The seal of the Bishop of Copenhagen quartered with the arms of the Diocese. Quarters 2 and 3 are identical with those of the famous convert, anatomist and Bishop, Niels Stensen, who first recognised the heart to be a muscle.

The arms of the Diocese of Copenhagen.

The wafer-seal of Leo Ferdinand Dworschak, Bishop of Fargo in North Dakota, U.S.A.

The seal of Pope John XXIII.

The seals of Archbishop Heim, Apostolic Delegate to Great Britain, and the Apostolic Delegation in London.

11) Canon 2056, § 1, commands the sealing of the original 'acta' which must be kept carefully in the diocesan archives, and which can no longer be opened without the express authorisation of the Holy See. Paragraph two requires, in the same way, the sealing of the *Transumptum* with the bishop's seal. A report of the sealing must be drawn up by the notary, in duplicate, one copy of which is sent to Rome and the other remains in the diocesan archives. The *sigillum ordinarii* mentioned here should differ from the *sigillum curiae* at least in its legend, and it must bear the arms of the bishop, while the other must bear the arms of the diocese, if such exist.

12) Canon 2063, § 3, is the most exacting of all with regard to the care of the seal. It obliges the bishop to send the Sacred Congregation of Rites (now the S. Congregation for the Causes of Saints) a description or a copy of the seal with which he has sealed the *transumptum* so that the authenticity of the letter may be verified with absolute certainty.

13) Canon 2073 finally, and in addition, anticipates (in the matter of the seals) that the Protonotary of the Sacred Congregation will examine the seals of the proceedings of the process of information which has been sent to Rome by the bishop. Only after this examination is it permitted to go ahead with the unsealing.

14) Given the great importance attributed to seals in canon law, as must be abundantly evident by now, it is natural that they are also mentioned in criminal law, where there are severe penalties for any forgery or abuse in the matter of ecclesiastical seals. Canon 2360, § 1, threatens anyone who counterfeits the documents of the Holy See, or knowingly uses such counterfeit documents, with excommunication *latae sententiae* and *speciali modo* reserved to the Holy See. Paragraph two of the same Canon lays down extra penalties should the delinquent be a cleric or a religious. In order to counterfeit a document it is clearly necessary either to counterfeit the seal as well, or to use it without proper authority.

15) Canon 2362 also threatens penalties for forgers of ecclesiastical documents issued by secondary authorities (see also Canon 2406).

16) Another very important use of the seal was prescribed by the Constitution *Vacante Sede Apostolica*
of Saint Pius X (December 25th, 1904). It concerns
the red seal with which the cardinals in conclave
should seal their ballots. The use of armorial seals
was here formally rejected as they would naturally
have betrayed the voter. The cardinals make use
of a secret seal, very simple in form, showing only
three numbers, letters or a figure. The secrecy thus
ensured could only be disclosed in the extreme case
of an election made on the bare required majority
when the cardinal elected would have been obliged
to reveal his seal to verify that he had not voted
for himself, thus determining his own election. This
instruction is outdated by now, the new order of the
Conclave excluding possibility of such an abuse.

The reform of the manner of election of the
Sovereign Pontiff introduced by the Constitution
Vacantis Apostolicae Sedis of Pius XII December
8th, 1945, now requires that the one elected obtain
two thirds of the votes, plus one. Thus if the legal
majority has been reached, nothing forces this unpleasant check to be made any longer. As a result
of this reform the ballots, which have been very
much simplified, no longer need to be signed or
sealed. The Apostolic Constitution "Romano Ponti-
fici Eligendo" of 1st October 1975 in no way
affects heraldic usage.

Almost all the ecclesiastical seals dealt with above are
armorial seals, or seals marked with emblems of
ecclesiastical rank, depicted in heraldic style.

Sometimes, especially where Papal Bulls are concerned,
the seals are engraved with the images of saints, or they
may be simple stamps with nothing more than a legend.

Canon Law provides for the two universally known
uses of seals – authentication of written documents, and
the official closure of letters, boxes, cabinets, cupboards,
doors, drawers, tombs, reliquaries and so on. To fulfil
the first purpose, an embossing press or rubber stamp
may be used; to fulfil the second it is necessary to use
a real wax seal.

The seal of Pope Paul VI.

*The seal of Cardinal Wendel, former
Archbishop of Munich.*

*Reliquary seal of Bishop Murphy-
O'Connor of Arundel and Brighton.*

29

The seals of Archbishop Gerald O'Hara, of Savannah, U.S.A., former Apostolic Delegate to Great Britain, and the seal of the Diocese of Savannah.

The seal of the Bishop of Chur.

THE COAT OF ARMS AS USED IN SEALS

The considerable importance that contemporary Canon Law continues to attribute to seals leads us to make an excursion into the field of diplomatics and sigillography.

The seal was already in daily use as a legal instrument in antiquity. The most ancient seals are those engraved with figures (sigillum means a little image, figure or relief).

Among the Anglo-Saxons, Franks, Alemanni and other peoples, seals were possessed by kings, bishops, dukes, counts, centurions and judges. The Popes had been using seals since the Sixth Century. Besides seals with figures, there were seals adorned with a simple legend or monogram, and, naturally, seals with both figures and legends.

In the Middle Ages, portrait seals representing the sealer were especially favoured. We can find in this important period, among other forms, the superb round equestrian seals.

Since the appearance of heraldic adornment on knights' armour, the portraits on seals have been likewise adorned. This type of seal came into being almost at the same time as the use of the coat of arms, which rapidly and universally became the characteristic element of the seal's image. The knights, pictured within the small dimensions of a seal, can only be distinguished from one another by the heraldic emblems on their armour. Step by step the stage was reached where all that was depicted was the heraldic emblem; in this way the arms were substituted for the portraits, and themselves became symbolic portraits.

It was, therefore, through the seal as a symbolic portrait and personal mark that armory became a symbol of power and authority, of authenticity and good faith. The armorial seal was an ideal instrument, offering fine images, of infinite variety, and easily identified, while being artistic, elegant and personal.

3

THE ECCLESIASTICAL SEALS

The oldest ecclesiastical seal – known from a description only – is that of Pope Agapetus (535-536). Original documents sealed by the Popes have been preserved since the Ninth Century. The ancient Papal Seals had the popes' names engraved on them. The seals on the Papal Bulls show on one side the heads or busts of SS. Peter and Paul, and on the other is engraved the name of the reigning Pope.

The Fisherman's Ring, which is used to seal briefs, bears the image of Saint Peter hauling his nets into his boat, and the name of the reigning Pope.

On the seals and stamps of the Roman Curia, the various departments of the Vatican and the Pontifical Institutes, there are, instead of arms, the heraldic insignia of the pontifical dignity : the tiara and keys.

By the time of the Merovingian Kings, bishops as well as dukes were permitted a limited use of seals. Before that, kings had considered it as a right exclusive to themselves. Seyler does not hesitate to declare bishops' seals as old as those of Kings, and it is certain that since the Tenth Century bishops have sealed secular documents.

Chapters, Abbeys and Monasteries began to use seals in the course of the Eleventh Century, and by the Twelfth Century prelates and canons possessed personal seals.

Ecclesiastics' seals were, at first, like those of others, portrait seals with half-length or whole figures. Seals depicting saints were also commonplace. Then came armorial seals, with the seal marks frequently surrounded by a legend. At the time of the introduction of armorial church seals, the shield was, at first, often placed at the feet of a figure. Soon, however, the arms dominated the field alone, and signs of dignity were added to the shield – first the crosier and the mitre. A little later the hat appeared, as a characteristic external ornament, on the seals of cardinals, and not long after on the seals of protonotaries and other prelates.

Those bishops who were at the same time temporal lords made use of the prelate's seal for their decrees of government, whether ecclesiastical or temporal. These

The seals of Bishop Hengsbach of Essen and of the Diocese of Essen which was created in 1957.

The seal of Bishop Edward Daly of Derry in Ireland.

The seals of Bishop René Boudon of Mende in France and the Diocese of Mende.

The seal, in form of a rubber stamp, of Mgr. John Edward Taylor, Bishop of Stockholm, b. in 1914 in East St. Louis, U.S.A.: consecrated bishop by the author in 1962; died 1976.

seals were often indistinguishable from those of feudal lords; many prelates, especially in Germany, preferred to adorn their shields with helms rather than hierarchical ornaments.

Since the end of the Thirteenth Century armorial bearings have more and more replaced the former seal marks, to such an extent that the word seal has almost become a synonym for coat of arms in some countries.

In the Middle Ages the validity of a document was often totally dependent on the seal as guarantee for authenticity. Later, an engraved representation of the arms was also put at the top of documents. This usage spread to official correspondence, and even to private correspondence, as a means of lending such papers an air of distinction and solemnity.

The importance of seals (and consequently of arms) has been affirmed time and again by Popes and legal authorities.

A decree of Alexander III, of 1166, prescribes that all documents presented at the Papal Court be sealed, and declares null and void, after the death of the witnesses, any written document not guaranteed by public authority or provided with an authentic seal. Princes of the Church, Bishops, chapters and temporal princes were among those who could affix authentic seals.

The canonist, Bernard of Pavia (d. 1213), attributes the public recognition of documents to the authentic seal. Tancrede of Bologna (d. 1236/8) is of the same opinion, as is also Pope Innocent IV (1234-54) in his commentaries on the Decretals.

Guillaume Durand (d. 1296) recounts that in the Roman Curia credence is only given to authentic seals, and admits public credence to the seals of cardinals, legates, archbishops and bishops, and their officials, princes, abbots nullius and notaries public.

Yet not all the commentators on ecclesiastical law are of the same opinion. Some dispute the power of the seal to give a public character to documents. But all grant that they afford strong convincing evidence, and officially this property is recognised in them until proof to the contrary.

Since the clergy commonly sealed secular documents as well, their seals enjoyed the protection of the state everywhere. In 1307, Edward I of England decreed that each monastery should have a seal and any unsealed paper was void and without legal effect.* The Council of London had, moreover, already prescribed in 1237 that not only the archbishops and bishops, but also their officials, abbots, priors, deans, archdeacons, rural deans, cathedral chapters, colleges, monasteries and their superiors, were all obliged to possess seals, for in the Kingdom of England there were no official court scriveners, and authentic seals were the more important because of that.

Given the great authority afforded to written documents in the Middle Ages, no one can be surprised at the profusion of documentary and seal forgeries. But it is surprising to discover with what ease these forgeries were made, and how ecclesiastics and religious, even with pious intentions, created documents out of nothing with the purpose of advancing a cause, or bringing off a claim, or raising the prestige of their monastery, their country or even their own family.

The forgers were surprisingly skilful and greatly varied their dodges. Pope Innocent III (1198-1216) lists and condemns nine different procedures.

The public authorities of past centuries had to wage a ceaseless war on these forgers, and applied stiff penalties to them; heavy fines, branding, exile and even death.

A cleric who forged a prince's seal was to be deposed, and, in addition, branded and exiled.

Anyone who forged a papal document, or caused one to be forged, was excommunicated, together with those who aided him, and if clerics were involved they suffered loss of offices and livings, and were unfrocked and handed over to the secular courts. The person who knowingly made use of a forgery was liable to like punishment.

To make forgeries more difficult, prelates and laymen often used a counter seal (*sigillum secretum*) which they applied on the reverse of their great seal (*sigillum authenticum, publicum*), thus confirming the latter.

For less important papers they used the little seal (*sigillum ad causas*), or privy seal. In former times, bishops sometimes used special seals between the time of their election and consecration; these did not display emblems of the episcopal order. Seals of bishops-elect have long since fallen into disuse.

To make documents even more authentic, and their forgery more difficult, the offices of the Holy See have

* Woodward, p. 4.

The seal of the Parish of Helsingborg in Sweden.

The seal, in form of a rubber stamp, of the Parish of Kreuzlingen in Switzerland; (designed by the author in 1940; stamp not engraved).

The rubber stamp seal of the Parish of Pfyn in Switzerland; (designed by the author; stamp not engraved).

The personal seal of the Cistercian Abbot Bernard Kaul.

The seal of the Abbey of Lilienfeld; the Abbey's canting arms are impaled with the canting arms of Abbot Mussbacher.

like many others long been using water-marks showing the insignia of papal dignity.

Heraldic water-marks, like armorial seals and stamps, will never be surpassed artistically and decoratively, and they have the double advantage, common to arms, of easy recognition and being personal to the user.

A comparison between the seals simply marked with initials, which the French bishops were forced to use between 1802-1808, and the beautiful armorial seals, allows one to see how coats of arms are elegant and decorative, having all the qualities desirable in seal images. During these years the bishops charged their shields with intertwined initials, adorned, nevertheless, with emblems of ecclesiastical rank. Hence the tiresome uniformity of monogrammed seals and difficulty in identification – the diversity of initials is not great, and even among a small number of people it happens that more than one person have the same initials. On the other hand, armorial bearings are not easily mistakable.

It is not possible to close this chapter without a very emphatic recommendation to the competent authorities, and to the engravers of seals, to give their most careful and thoughtful attention to the art of the seal and ecclesiastical stamp. A seal should be an ornament but, unhappily, negligence and bad taste have resulted in many seals and stamps lacking all artistic worth. They mar a document instead of beautifying it and adding to its solemnity.

Left: The seal of Pope Paul VI made in Rome. Right: The seal of Pope Paul which is now in use, engraved by Rudolf Niedballa, after precisely the same design by the author.

34

II

THE USE OF ARMS ON VATICAN COINS
AND POSTAL STAMPS

The obverse and reverse of a coin showing the arms of Pope Pius VII; he impaled his family arms with those of the Benedictine Order.

A second function of arms, of less moment for the universal Church, is their use as ornaments on the coins of the Vatican State. We cannot introduce a treatise on Vatican numismatics at this point. Those who desire to know more about this subject would do well to read the excellent work of Camillo Serafini*. These coins can serve as useful guides to certain basic points.

Since the non-military use of armory became customary, temporal sovereigns and popes have liked to have coins struck bearing their arms. They are thus marked with the emblems of the authority which puts them into circulation and guarantees that they are legal currency. Arms have become so significant in numismatics that in the Papal States and elsewhere large silver coins have taken on the name of "scudi" (écus, escudos, i.e. shields).

With the help of the Papal coins we can follow, at least in part, the evolution of the Papal arms. The coins of Alexander V (1409-1415) and his predecessors were not marked with arms, but with the tiara and the keys in various guises. The coins of the Anti-pope, John XXIII (1410-1415), are the first to bear an armorial shield, stamped with the triple-crowned tiara. Martin V (1417-1431) was the first Pope to stamp his coins with his family arms surmounted by the tiara and keys. Since that time there has been no change; the Papal Arms have attained their fixed and definitive composition.

Vatican postage stamps; the cancellation also includes heraldry.

After the abolition of the Papal States, the pontifical mint (zecca) ceased its activity, and the Popes no longer had anything coined save commemorative medals, without monetary value but still with the papal arms.

Following the reconciliation between the Vatican and Italy, and the reconstitution of a sovereign Papal State, Papal coins began to circulate again; they are legal tender in Italy as well. The arms of the reigning Pope are stamped on the reverse of the coins, as of old, with the tiara and keys.

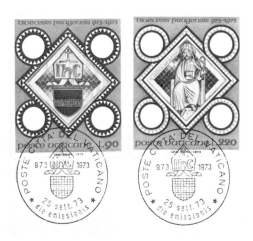

* Le monete e le bolle plumbee del medagliere Vaticano, Milano 1910-1913.

The first coins to be issued *sede vacante* date from the year 1378. Some of them show a mitre or tiara; others are stamped with a cross patty, in the angles of which one can make out two pairs of keys in saltire and two mitres or tiaras.

The coins *sede vacante* of 1394 have the tiara on the obverse and the keys in saltire on the reverse. The basilical pavilion appears for the first time during the interregnum of 1521, marshalled with the arms of Cardinal Armellini. The first *sede vacante* coins to be issued after the solution of the Roman question, as of old, bear the arms of the Cardinal Camerlengo (in this case Cardinal Pacelli, later Pope Pius XII), marshalled with the pavilion and keys.

Some of the stamps of the New Vatican Postal Service bear the arms of the Pope, while others show the keys in saltire, like the stamps issued before 1870.

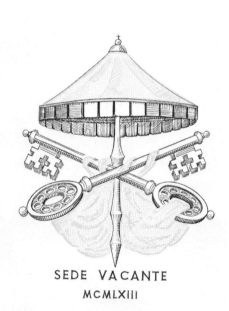

SEDE VACANTE
MCMLXIII

First Day Cover *Roma.*

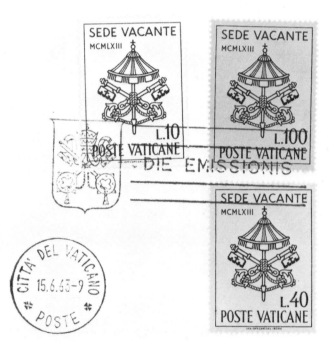

This envelope depicts the stamps, design and cancellation used while the Throne of St. Peter was vacant after the death of Pope John XXIII and before the election of Pope Paul VI.

36

III

THE USE OF ARMS IN ECCLESIASTICAL ART

For centuries decorative art has used the motifs of heraldry very frequently. The façades and interiors of churches, and other buildings belonging to the church, are often adorned with arms. One can find them on quite varied articles of worship, such as chalices. As well as being decorative, arms serve to recall former owners or donors or to keep historical memories alive.

Over the main door of all churches in Rome, the palaces of the Roman Congregations, Pontifical Institutes, Apostolic Nunciatures, and Delegations throughout the world, the arms of the Holy See or the reigning Pope are affixed symbolising his power as Supreme Pontiff and Monarch, and the Church's legal rights to the building.

Those churches in Rome which are titularities of Cardinals, show the arms of their Cardinals according to a formal decree of the Congregation of Ceremonies dated 7th September, 1658, the arms being considered as a sign of their pre-eminence and dignity. For the same reason, in many dioceses, the bishop's arms are displayed on the façades of churches and above the bishop's throne in cathedrals.

Unfortunately, for the most part, these arms are so badly produced and of such inferior design, from the heraldic as well as the artistic point of view, that one hesitates to mention them in a chapter which deals with coats of arms in ecclesiastical art.

However many famous churches and palaces have their façades and interiors resplendent with Papal and ecclesiastical arms which are *chefs-d'oeuvre* of monumental art, and which give a visible testimony to the leading role that Popes have played as inspirers and protectors of the Arts. The Renaissance and Baroque periods produced truly imposing works of architectural heraldic art. While giving free rein to our admiration, we have to point out how far removed these styles are from the pristine simplicity of early living heraldry.

Heraldic ornaments have been placed almost everywhere in churches. Ceilings, floors, doors, gratings, walls, altars, plinths, choir-stalls, windows, lamps, candlesticks,

Tapestry from the apartments of Pope John XXIII with his coat of arms.

Reliquary decorated with coats of arms, made by Egino Weinert, the well known ecclesiastical artist in Cologne, Germany.

37

Two armorial medallions depicting papal arms.

The tomb of Adrian VI, r.1522-23, the last non-Italian Pope.

chalices, church-banners and even liturgical vestments; all have provided magnificent opportunities for diverse artists and craftsmen to display their talents.

Coats of arms, ablaze with the splendour of their colours, may be considered as works of art in their own right. Yet very often they are tucked away in the corner of some picture or window in memory of their donors.

Many are the liturgical books that bear the arms of the Popes who decreed their publication, or those of the prelate who gave his *imprimatur* to them, thus making their authenticity more visible. (An *imprimatur* is an official declaration that the book contains nothing against faith or morals and may therefore be published).

It is not only in the churches of Rome that one comes across this profusion of heraldic ornament. It can be seen throughout the whole world, in cathedrals, in abbeys, smaller churches and even the smallest of chapels. Arms which adorn the tombs in churches and cemeteries (subject to Canon Law) may also be considered as part of the Church's heraldic usage.

By no means all these coats of arms belong to ecclesiastics. Many lay arms have found their way into churches through patronage, foundation or donation. Thus our sanctuaries have become real museums of the art of heraldry. If anyone wants proof let him observe its manifestations in those ancient churches which escaped the destruction of revolutionary vandalism.

In this chapter the legal point of view must be considered with the artistic. Should the display of coats of arms be allowed in churches and on objects of liturgical usage? Are they merely tolerated, or should they be banned?

For centuries, as we have seen, people have ceased to be offended by the military origins of heraldry, and today arms, in a sacred place, represent people who have some lawful position in the Church – be they members of the Hierarchy, or simple baptised members of the Christian community – and so they should not be excluded *a priori* from consecrated places, vessels and ornaments. We are very aware that besides being a source of legitimate pride, arms may also be the object of foolish vanity, and we have no wish to plead here for caste prejudice. Anything may be abused, and no one can blame the arms for their eventual misuse.

Without indulging in the excessive over-zeal of some Seventeenth Century Zürich pastors, who engaged in an obstinate struggle lasting many years to banish the arms of distinguished laymen from the church benches, it has to be admitted that there is a use of coats of arms which can be considered as improper in a church, namely when its main purpose is simply to secure the best seats for certain individuals.

The case is different where the arms belong to clergy, or those laity who are patrons, founders or donors, and provide a general service to the Church.

What then is the juridical status of arms in churches?

On the 26th March, 1924, the Sacred Congregation of Rites brought into force an instruction dated 15th December, 1922, which concerned the introduction of flags into churches. This instruction contained a decision of principle. It permitted the introduction of flags into church, even if they were not blessed, on the condition that they did not belong to associations which are openly hostile to the Church, and that they did not depict the unacceptable, as, for example, obscene figures, or anti-religious emblems.

Moreover, there is a strong case to be made, by way of custom, for the presence of armory in churches; this is not difficult to establish for the old Law often showed itself as positively favourable. For example, it is permitted to have arms on the tombs in churches. Patrons of churches have the right to display their own arms in the churches.

Upon examining the acts of the Rota, the Congregation of Bishops, and of the former Congregation of Rites, many interesting decisions can be found to prove that the Holy See protected the arms which adorned churches. There is no need to enumerate all the examples; they confirm absolutely what has already been stated, as a few make clear:

A bishop cannot remove arms which have been put in a church to commemorate his predecessors, especially if they have been put there at the latters' expense. Similarly, arms are permitted on liturgical vestments and on liturgical objects, whether it be in memory of the donors or as a mark of ownership.

Patrons, benefactors and all those who contributed to the building, or the ornamentation of a church, have the

The arms of Pope Pius X carved in a Vatican ceiling and two cherubs supporting the papal tiara and keys.

The arms of Pope Urban VIII on the base of the Baldichino column of the papal altar in St Peter's, Rome.

The arms of Pius IX on the base of a lamp in St Peter's Square, Rome.

right to put their arms on it. It is just possible that, seeing these, other donors will be encouraged . . . but in such a case it is wise not to examine the purity of intention too closely! The great mystic, Johannes Tauler (d. 1361), was of the opinion that donors' arms are a vain exhibition in a church, and he made a point of telling the owners that they were thus sufficiently rewarded for their good works.

Saint Charles Borromeo (d. 1584) was an adversary of coats of arms. As Archbishop and Cardinal he never bore his family arms, and did not wish to see them displayed anywhere in his diocese. At a diocesan synod he forbade the display of arms on liturgical vestments and in holy places, and he ordered the removal of all those which had been so placed within the previous seven years, save for those on tombs.

In spite of such isolated and local prohibitions, the supreme ecclesiastical authority has never declared itself against the custom of placing armorial bearings in churches. On the contrary, it has permitted the affixing of arms to walls, doors and belfries of churches and chapels; the same applies to altars and baptismal fonts.

Arms are allowed as marks of patronal rights, but obviously with the permission of the competent prelate. Without special authorisation it is forbidden to display armorial bearings in churches, as is the case with other forms of adornment. It is important to keep in mind the need for discipline concerning the admission of arms, for their presence in a church could serve to affirm and prove patronal rights, and arguably constitute a presumptive right in favour of their owners.

It is impossible nowadays in the Roman Catholic Church to revive patronal rights, where their exercise has ceased, on the grounds of arms situated in a church or chapel. Canon 1455, section 3, still allows, however, holders of the right of patronage permission to display their family arms in their churches. But since patronage is not the only reason permitting one to place armorial bearings in a church, the simple fact of the presence of family arms does not meet the requirements of Canon 1454 for the admission of patronal rights. This presence, together with other facts, could nonetheless serve as an argument supplementing the proofs.

The legislation of the Code on the right of patronage reveals a clear tendency to eliminate this institution as

Right:

The four 'Pius Windows' in Cologne Cathedral, executed by Wilhelm Geyer. They depict the Popes Pius IX, X, XI and XII with their coats of arms.

Below:

The designs for the papal arms by the author.

Bottom right:

The arms of Pope John XXIII on a church bell.

much as possible, for, in the past, it seriously restricted the bishops' freedom of action. If all the old arms found in churches could serve as arguments with which to establish patronal rights they would indeed frustrate the Church's intention of eliminating lay patronage.

The Code will not allow new patronal rights (Canon 1450 § 1), and thus this cause of past opposition to arms in churches has disappeared for ever.

Further, it is no longer permitted to erect new tombs within a church, except in the case of a Pope, a member of the royal family, a cardinal, bishop, abbot or prelate *nullius* (Canon 1205 § 2).

Thus, there were but three titles to the admission of lay arms in church; the right of patronage, burial and donation. As far as the future is concerned, the first two have been abolished; the third still stands.

A Bull seal, reproduced as a medal, depicting SS Peter and Paul.

CHAPTER THREE
I

HERALDIC LAW WITHIN THE FRAMEWORK OF CANON LAW

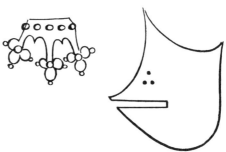

To study the Heraldic Law of the Church methodically, we must first examine primary and fundamental questions.

How did the Church, whose purpose is the sanctification of mankind, come to provide itself with an heraldic law and how is it, a worldly matter, made compatible with Canon Law?

It is necessary to distinguish the heraldic law of the Church from that of secular heraldry; to show its connection with the regulations concerning pontifical insignia and ornaments; and to study those particular external ornaments, recognised in public law, which are peculiar to ecclesiastical arms.

Having reached the heart of our subject we must scrutinise first the legal principles that govern the acquisition and loss of the right to bear ecclesiastical arms depending from the law concerning offices and livings. Only then will it be possible to aggregate clearly the body of heraldic laws so far promulgated by the Holy See.

In foregoing chapters the many and varied forms of heraldic art used in the Church have been touched upon in brief. The classic art of identifying individuals and corporations in an expressive and lucid way has been employed by the Hierarchy for more than Seven Centuries. Beyond its ornamental uses heraldry, as already explained, has a fundamental legal application and thus necessarily found its place within the system of Canon Law.

Seal of the Bishop of Bayeux, c.1164.

This study is confined to the law and custom of church heraldry, and covers nothing but the armorial bearings of clergy, religious orders and ecclesiastical institutes.

Coats of arms, as we have said before, represent persons and corporate bodies. The ornaments outside the shield indicate their rank and dignity; this makes for easy identification of all grades in the Hierarchy, and is of great practical service.

The heraldic law of the Church, which is based on the dogmatic and in part only juridical and historical order of the Hierarchy, is exclusively connected with ecclesiastical status. The right of knighthood was founded, in the early days of heraldry, first on military service and then on birth, whereas ecclesiastical status is derived from ordination or consecration and the exercise of an ecclesiastical office, or, for the religious, from profession and later election to a higher office. In the Church birth plays no decisive role.

Ecclesiastical heraldry is not determined by heraldic considerations alone, but also by doctrinal, liturgical and canonical factors. It not only produces arms denoting members of the ecclesiastical state, but shows the rank of the bearer.

According to its constitution, established by Our Lord himself, the Church is an hierarchical organisation made up of elders and subordinates.

The heraldry of the Church, therefore, aims at reflecting this clear and indisputable representation of the hierarchy of divine and ecclesiastical law, and to this end the ecclesiastical law of heraldry is a special part of the internal positive law of the Church.

To depict ecclesiastical rank, heraldic art uses liturgical ornaments and insignia, notably headgear, as does secular heraldry when it makes use of helmets, crowns and caps as badges of rank. We should, however, note one difference : coat-armour was worn as living heraldry only in times long past; crowns of nobility (excepting those of sovereigns and British peers) are almost never worn, whereas the insignia of ecclesiastics are still in effective use.

These insignia or marks of dignity belong to the persons either by inherent right (for example, the mitre and crozier of bishops), or else by virtue of privileges which are recognised by common law (for example, the abbot's mitre and crozier).

The arms of Dr. John Tanner show how two chivalric Orders of ecclesiastical origin, Knight Commander of St Gregory the Great and Commander of the Venerable Order of St John, may be artistically deployed in conjunction with personal arms.

The arms of Cardinal Michele Pellegrino, former Archbishop of Turin.

Commemorative medals are struck in each year of a Pontificate. Illustrated here are the medals of the first year of the reign of Popes Pius XII, John XXIII and Paul VI.

As a result, the heraldic law of the Church is in many respects within the competence of the Sacred Congregation of Divine Worship. This same Congregation is authorised to grant insignia and privileges of honour, either personal and limited in duration, or real and perpetual. In addition, the Sacred Congregation of Divine Worship has the task of watching over privileges concerning sacred rites and of suppressing any abuse which might tend to spread (Canon 253 § 2).

In spite of its inherent spirituality and supernatural purpose the Church has the right, as a true, visible, hierarchical and juridically perfect society, and by virtue of its administrative powers, to devise ranks, to establish new offices, and to confer on their incumbents distinctive insignia of honour as marks of dignity.

Only the purpose of the Church limits its legislative power. This power extends to everything which directly or indirectly facilitates the activity of the Church, whose aim is to guarantee the common good of the faithful in view of their eternal destination. The Church cannot allow any evil practice, owing to its moral and spiritual rôle, and, as said before, if arms derived from its authority appear to be used solely for vain and pretentious reasons this constitutes an abuse by the user and cannot be held as condemnation of ecclesiastical heraldry *per se,* the general usefulness of which cannot be gainsaid.

It is, moreover, obvious that even outside the divine service liturgical vestments and other emblems of ecclesiastical dignity have representative, administrative and ornamental functions which are closely connected with the essential work of the Church. The distinction between members of the Hierarchy, which heraldry shows, as do vestments, is in no way a private affair. On the contrary, it is ruled by ancient customs and special legislation.

The Church specifically cannot permit the uncontrolled use, at the whim of any individual or corporation of those signs which denote the various offices of the Hierarchy.

44

II

ECCLESIASTICAL AND CIVIL HERALDIC LAW

The Church's Heraldic Law is concerned primarily with the use of Hierarchical insignia. The Church has neither interest nor reason to go further, and is not concerned with the family arms which many clergy have inherited and continue to bear, adding the emblem of their own ecclesiastical status and rank; nor with the arms of clerics who, not being armigerous, assume arms when they are raised to a dignity.

These latter may devise for themselves charges and tinctures with which to decorate their shields, according to the rules of the herald's art. The Church neither prescribes nor proscribes in this matter. Churchmen have only to conform with the laws of their respective countries, which mostly allow them complete latitude in this matter. Yet, in some countries, as in Great Britain, the adoption of arms is subject to an official authority, the College of Arms, which levies a fee. This was also the case in the Austrian Empire. Under the French Empire, bishops were ennobled and had the right to their own arms with the emblems of their noble dignity in a 'franc-quartier' and to transmit title and arms to a nephew.

In the eyes of the Church it is sufficient to determine who has the right to bear an ecclesiastical coat of arms and under what conditions the different insignia are acquired or lost.

Because of the extensive official use of ecclesiastical heraldry, and because of the general ignorance in this respect, it would perhaps be useful to register and check the new arms of bishops and prelates who have to use official seals. This would not be done to delimit the choice of arms but simply to avoid heraldic blunders. The choice of prelatical arms is often a disastrous defiance of the rules of heraldry, if only as a breach of good taste. This regrettable situation ensured that, under the pontificate of Pius X, new bishops in Italy were invited to seek the advice of the *Collegio Araldico,* officially established (1853) under the pontificate of Pius IX, and still existing in Rome as a private Academy.

Mgr. Pierre-Marie Gerlier was granted the pallium as Bishop of Tarbes and Lourdes. Later he became Archbishop of Lyon and a Cardinal. The shield is overcharged and the decorative flowers surrounding the ill-placed pallium are heraldically insupportable.

The arms of Abbot Don Joseph Bourigan, being an example of the heraldry against which the author warns throughout his text.

Ecclesiastical heraldry also ignores the armorial bearings conferred by Popes with titles of nobility. This activity has nothing to do with the government of the Church directly, nor does it concern the clergy. The Popes conferred these titles and arms as heads of state, rather than as pontiffs of the Universal Church. Following the loss of the Papal States they continued this practice until some twenty years ago by virtue of their unchallenged position as Sovereigns in international law. Thus, this matter is the concern of the nobiliary and heraldic jurisdictions of various countries to establish laws relative to the admission and use of titles and coats of arms granted by a foreign power, or more correctly, by a sovereign of supranational status.

III

ECCLESIASTICAL HERALDIC LAW AND THE RIGHT TO PONTIFICAL INSIGNIA

1420

In general, the shield with its partitions and charges is the subject of the science and art of heraldry. This is no concern of the Church. Its attention is focussed on the external ecclesiastical ornaments only, which accompany or surround the shield. Only from the form of the shield (the oval and lozenge being reserved by preference for women – although this custom is not always observed), it might be possible to recognize whether one is looking at the arms of a man or a woman. Clerical arms become evident when certain conventional marks – the external ornaments – are added outside the shield.

At the dawn of heraldry the shields and helmets worn by the knights had no distinctive marks showing differences of rank. Even in the Thirteenth Century the crowns adorning the helmet generally played a merely decorative role. The use of crowns indicating rank did not begin until the Fourteenth Century in England, France and Italy. Later it spread to Germany. Since the Seventeenth Century these crowns have been figured according to fixed rules, and indicate precisely, at a glance, the different titles of nobility.

46

These crowns were alien to primitive heraldry. They have, naturally, differed in style and form from country to country. Church dignitaries have not been slow to help themselves to crowns, at times marshalling them thoughtlessly with ecclesiastical insignia. To end this sort of abuse Innocent X forbade the use of crowns for Cardinals (D. 1.) and Benedict XV had to apply the same prohibition to bishops (and, implicitly, to all prelates) (D. 16.).

Nevertheless it was necessary to characterize ecclesiastical arms in some way. Which symbols ought one to choose? The helmet denoted that the bearer was a warrior, the crown presented him as a noble. Neither helmet nor crown befits a priest and prelates quickly made use of a liturgical headpiece to ensign their shields. The mitre quite naturally became the characteristic mark of the bishop, and was soon adopted by other prelates privileged with the use of pontifical insignia.

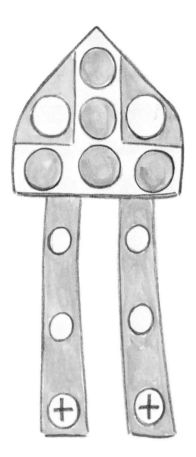

The famous English chronicler, Matthew of Paris (1195-1259), a monk of Cluny, in his *Historia minor Anglorum*, furnished with heraldic illustrations, was the first to mark ecclesiastical arms by adding liturgical insignia to them. In the passage dealing with the death of William of Provence, who died in 1239 as bishop-elect of Valence and Liège, he put in the margin of the manuscript an inverted shield with crozier and two mitres (two mitres because of the two dioceses; later, to signify jurisdiction over two territories, two croziers were preferred). The mitre and crozier are found in other places as marginal illustrations. The cross, the tiara, represented as a conical bonnet, the papal pavilion and other ecclesiastical insignia are also to be found. Matthew of Paris does not, at this date, show the Cardinal's Hat – it was adopted into heraldry later.

Just as in a portrait a bishop is vested with his pontifical insignia, his arms – being a symbolic portrait – are decked with such marks of dignity.

Pontifical insignia are proper to bishops; other dignitaries possess them by privilege alone. Thus, according to canon law, their use was permitted to Cardinals even if they were not bishops (C.239 § 1, 13°), to abbots and prelates *nullius* (C.325), and to abbots regular (C.625).

Certain prelates, even canons, at times have the restricted privilege of using pontifical insignia, subject to suitable restrictions. (D.2., D.3., D.15., nos. 5-6).

The arms of Mgr. de Marguerye, once a bishop of Autun, typifies many aspects of indifferent heraldry. Note, for example, that there are three items of head-gear, hat, mitre and crown, all of differing sizes although intended for the same head. The pallium is very ill-placed.

The granting of such privileges is the exclusive prerogative of the Holy See. In the introduction to the *Motu proprio, Inter multiplices curas,* which is the most important document in the heraldic law of the Church (D.15), Saint Pius X declared that one of the many duties of his apostolic functions was to protect the pontifical privileges of the bishops. He deplored the fact that either through wrong intention, or a false or too lax interpretation, the discipline of the Church had not been observed and episcopal dignity had been harmed. In spite of the many protests and prescriptions of his predecessors (Alexander VII, Benedict XIV, Pius VII and Pius IX), the use of insignia and prerogatives had become excessively widespread, through ambition and devious subterfuge, thus allowing unauthorized clerics to encroach upon the dignity of genuine pontiffs.

To correct such infringements Saint Pius X decided, after consulting with canonists and liturgists, that prelates below the rank of bishop have no rights to insignia which are not named in the *motu proprio* – which deals also with the insignia authorized as heraldic marks of dignity.

Henceforth no cleric was allowed to use a liturgical sign as an external heraldic ornament unless proper to his function and dignity. On the other hand it would be impracticable and *outré* to surround a shield with all the liturgical ornaments worn during religious functions. Simplicity was in the mind of the Church and, to repeat a basic premise, is one of the first qualities of classic heraldic art.

The heraldry of the Church has followed the same decadence in fashion as worldly heraldry. Departing from the fair and living realism* of its beginnings, it fell progressively into affectation and fantasy, often inspired by the bent of ostentation.

Also, the old design of the cardinal's hat, which at first had the shape of a medieval pilgrim's hat, was disfigured according to contemporary taste. It was no longer alone in adorning a cardinal's shield, as at first, but suffered the addition of many useless accessories.

The heraldic law of the Church tries to abolish that which is superfluous. The characteristic external

---

* That is not to say that its style was that of Realism; but that early heraldry depicted arms as they were in fact borne.

48

ornament expressing the dignity of the bearer must be dominant. The addition of different emblems with identical signification is to be avoided, and is now forbidden. The custom in the Roman Curia was often much more severe than the written law in this regard.

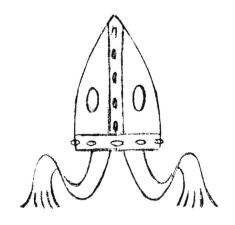

IV

THE HERALDIC INSIGNIA OF HIERARCHICAL DIGNITY AND OTHER ORNAMENTS EMPLOYED IN ECCLESIASTICAL ACHIEVEMENTS

To show the different ranks and offices of the clergy, ecclesiastical heraldry uses signs which by their connections with the Hierarchy, liturgy and canon law, impart a remarkable wealth of symbolism.

In general, these signs of dignity indicate spiritual authority. Some symbolize sacred order; others jurisdiction, or simply a certain ecclesiastical power; yet others mark but a rank of honour within the Hierarchy.

We must now study each of these emblems of clerical dignity used in the art of heraldry.

1

THE TIARA

The most exalted of these symbols is the tiara, emblem of the Papacy.

In olden days it was called a *regnum*, like the crowns of emperors and kings. The term *triregno* is still in use in Italy.

The tiara is an extra-liturgical headpiece of the Pope, which he wears on occasions of great solemnity and formerly in processions or parades. Scholars do not always agree on its origin. It was in any case originally a bonnet which underwent a long evolution to reach

Pope John XXIII wearing the Triple Tiara.

its present majestic form. It is difficult to prove it comes from this or that particular form of hat. Be that as it may, it is generally held now that the tiara comes from the *camelaucum* or *phrygium,* which was a white bonnet in the shape of a sugar-loaf, originating in the Orient and regarded in Rome as an emblem of liberty.

Others would relate the tiara with the High Priest's head-dress in the Old Testament, and to the mitre. It is certain, however, that there is no connection with the former, whilst one might admit that originally there was close resemblance to the mitre, which has also undergone a great deal of evolution.

The claim that the Phrygian cap was conferred on Pope Sylvester I (314-337) by the Emperor Constantine, as a sign of the freedom of the Church, has only the value of a legend. By this time the Popes certainly had a head-dress. The interesting question is when did it assume a particular meaning? It is certain that from about the Seventh Century the Popes wore a special headpiece as a sign of their eminent dignity.

Du Puy Demportes states that Pope Symmacus (498-514) wore a crown on his mitre. Nowadays it is supposed that the lower circlet of the tiara made its appearance only between the Ninth and Eleventh Centuries. Héfélé claims that the Popes started to decorate the bishop's mitre with a prince's crown when they became sovereigns; that is, in the time of Charlemagne, which seems a reasonable presumption; the fact remains, however, that no trace of such usage can be found in art before the Thirteenth Century.

The second crown was added to the tiara by Boniface VIII (1294-1303), one to represent spirtual and the other temporal power. We do not know whether or not this is Boniface's own interpretation!

The third crown was added under Benedict XI (1303-4) or Clement V (1305-1314). The triple-crowned tiara is mentioned for the first time in an inventory of the Papal Treasury dating from 1315.

Since then it has always appeared in that form as a symbol of Papal authority. Since about the Thirteenth Century it has had two ribbons, which were originally black, hanging from the back, like on a mitre.

The knob and small cross on the top of the tiara do not feature anywhere on the tombs of medieval Popes. It seems that these ornaments did not appear until the

Fifteenth Century. They are found for the first time on the precious tiara of Julius II (1503-1513). Unfortunately, we only have its picture left to us. The jewels which adorned it were handed over to pay for war indemnities, imposed in 1799 on the Pope by Bonaparte in the name of the Republic.

As Galbreath so rightly says,* the tiara has nothing to do with religious worship. Cardinal Saint Robert Bellarmine (1542-1621) and the heraldist, Giulio Cesare de Beatiano, were of the same opinion in their time, although Du Puy Demportes contradicts them. For him the tiara is a symbol of spiritual power and not at all the symbol of temporal power. The argument advanced by Beatiano in favour of his assertion that the tiara signifies temporal power is not firmly based. He writes daringly that the three crowns represent the three parts of the then known world: Europe, Asia and Africa. Why then should not two other crowns have been added later for America and Australia? Despite the weakness of his proposition it accords well with contemporary thought.

It is certain that when exercising liturgical functions the Pope wears the mitre and never the tiara. It, therefore, may positively be concluded that the latter is not a scacred headpiece, but rather a sign of the sovereign power of the Pope, both as Supreme Head of the Church and as ruler of the Papal State. The need to symbolise the unity of these two powers certainly guided the evolution of the tiara. It is possible to hold that the significance of temporal power was the prime motive for the creation of such a majestic crown, but now the special symbolism for the tiara is that of primacy over the Universal Church, and it would remain just as significant even if the temporal power were once again to disappear completely.

In the course of the coronation ceremony, the Cardinal-Proto-Deacon places the tiara on the head of the Sovereign Pontiff saying:

"Accipe tiaram tribus coronis ornatam; et scias te esse Patrem Principum et Regum, Rectorem Orbis, in terra Vicarium Salvatoris nostri Jesu Christi, Cui est honor et gloria in saecula saeculorum".

The pontifical triple crown can also symbolize not only the supremacy of the Pope over the three churches:

* Papal Heraldry p. 17.

The medal commemorating the Coronation of Pope John XXIII with the tiara on the reverse.

Pope Paul VI wearing the Mitra Preciosa.

Pope Boniface VIII (1294-1303), wearing the double-crown tiara, blessing an assembly. Clearly shown are the pavilion, the keys and the shield of arms.

Opposite:

Pope John XXIII, blessing Urbi et Orbi, with his coat of arms on a tapestry.

militant, penitent and triumphant, but also his triple ministry as priest, pastor and teacher of the faithful.

The first Pope to use the tiara as an external ornament for his shield was John XXII (1316-1334). The arms decorating the tomb of Pope Lucius III (1181-1185) at Verona, were added some 200 years after his death.

The rare heraldic usurpations of the tiara are themselves an indirect confirmation of its symbolizing the sovereignty and dignity of the Popes. It is helpful to know something of such usurpations.

Woodward points out that in the Abbey Church of Saint Athanasius at Pennabilli, the arms on the tomb of Bishop Robert Adimari of Montefeltro (d. 1484) are adorned with a single-crown tiara. The tomb and the arms are described by Ughelli, but it seems that this is only a mitre adorned with a count's crown. As the dignity of Count was conferred on the Bishops of Montefeltro by the Emperor Frederick II this instance is accounted for; besides, at this period the pontifical tiara had had three crowns for a long time, and the Bishops of Montefeltro were not the only bearers of a crowned mitre. The Bishops of Durham, in England, who were Counts Palatine, had one such on their helmets, as their magnificent equestrian seals show.* More than a Century earlier the Archbishops of Benevento had proudly arrayed themselves with a veritable tiara. Pope Paul II (1464-1471) put an end to this abuse.

Even recently the Patriarchs of Lisbon still bore a triple-crowned tiara. This is one of the most recent of Patriarchates, dating from November 7th, 1716. It is said that the tiara was conceded to the Patriarch shortly afterwards by Pope Clement XII (1730-1740). In spite of the most detailed research, we have not succeeded in finding proof of this assertion, and, according to our knowledge, there is no authentic document in existence concerning it, even in Lisbon. Thus it is by no means certain that this usage was introduced with the formal consent of Rome. Galbreath expresses the opinion that the Holy See has neither authorised nor opposed it, and doubtless he is right, for how could Rome have made such a concession?

On the other hand, it is easy to see why Rome has

* Greenwell and Blair, pl. 52.

not reacted in this matter, since it is not a factor which touches the essence of the Faith. King John V of Portugal (1707-1750) was known to have a marked tendency to obtain, for his Patriarch, the maximum of prestige and honour. Without schismatic intentions, he wished to make of Lisbon a kind of western Rome. The *sedia gestatoria* (sedan chair) and many other attributes of the Sovereign Pontiff were imitated there, in addition to the tiara.

Clement XII promised in 1737 that the Patriarch of Lisbon would always be elevated to the purple at the first consistory after his appointment, and granted him precedence even before the Legates *a latere*. Pius VI renewed the privileges granted by Clement XII on the occasion of a new nomination to the Patriarchal See in 1778; but both are silent on the subject of the tiara. The present Patriarch of Lisbon does not use the tiara neither in liturgy nor in heraldry, but his immediate predecessor still did.

Finally, another case of the usurpation of the tiara is cited by Count de Saint-Saud. It concerns Cardinal Antoine-Anne-Jules de Clermont-Tonnerre (d. 1830), whose seal showed the tiara over the shield. Saint-Saud expresses the opinion that the tiara may have been conceded to the Clermont-Tonnerre family at the same time as the keys appear as charges in his coat of arms.*

However, to bear the tiara and keys as charges within the shield is quite different from having them over the shield. On the shield they are ordinary charges only; outside, they are signs of dignity. It seems virtually impossible that a Pope could ever have conferred on someone, no matter whom, the right to make use of the tiara as an external ornament to their arms. Therefore, the use of the tiara by this Cardinal may be considered an aberration.

---

* Galbreath considers these keys as canting arms: Clermont. To justify usage of the tiara the Cardinal claimed that Pope Nicholas II (1059-1061) belonged to his family; but that would not permit him to adorn his own arms in the manner of a Pope.

The coronation medal of Pope Paul V.I, with tiara and keys on the reverse.

THE KEYS

In the Thirteenth Century the keys first appeared by themselves on church banners, seals and coins, then within the shields, and beside the shields of the Popes, and, finally, in saltire above or behind the shields. The origin and symbolism of these keys goes back to the founder of the Church Himself. The keys designate the supernatural power to bind and loose accorded by the Saviour to Peter and his successors. They are the metaphorical expression of the absolute authority of Christ, which is transmitted to Peter, His Vicar on earth, having power over the whole Church.

The Keys, therefore, symbolize the full power to administer the treasures of redemption, merited by Christ, and to teach His doctrine with authority. The words about the keys of the Kingdom of Heaven are addressed only to Peter, and since the Fifth Century at least, Peter, and he alone of all the Apostles, has been represented in Christian art with the keys as insignia of supreme power.

The symbolism of the keys is brought out in an ingenious and interpretative fashion by heraldic art. One of the keys is of gold (or), the other of silver (argent). The golden key, which points upwards on the dexter side, signifies the power which extends even to Heaven. The silver key, which must point up to the sinister side, symbolizes the power over all the faithful on earth. The two are often linked by a cordon Gules as a sign of the union of the two powers. The handles are turned downwards, for they are in the hand of the Pope, Christ's lieutenant on earth. The wards point upwards, for the power of binding and loosing engages Heaven itself. Finally, the wards are cut out in the shape of a cross, to recall that the Pope possesses his power through the death of Christ. (*Plate 5; No. 20*).

Only the tiara is placed on the catafalque of a deceased Pope. When the Holy See is vacant, the keys pass to the Cardinal-Camerlengo, who bears them in saltire beneath the *Pavilion*, behind or above his shield.

54

It is he who must watch over the rights of the Holy See until the election of a new Pope.

In the mass of literature consulted, only one case of wrong use of the keys was found. The shield of Monsignor X. G. R. Casanelli d'Istria, Bishop of Ajaccio (d. 1869) was seen by Count de Saint-Saud with the two keys behind it in saltire.

3

THE PAVILION

The pavilion carried before the Pope, from a wood-engraving in 'Das Concilium'.

Another emblem peculiar to the heraldry of the Church is the basilical pavilion, also called an "ombrellino"* (umbrella or canopy). It is recognized as an emblem of the Church, and is currently represented on its banners.

Although the Pope never uses it as an heraldic ensign, the pavilion constitutes a pontifical emblem. It has the shape of a half-open parasol, Gyronny of Gules and Or, with a border of these colours counter-changed. The staff is Or. It is considered as an ensign of the Roman Church and its temporal power. Since the Cardinal-Camerlengo supervises these powers, during a vacancy of the Holy See, he uses this symbol and places the two keys beneath it as a further act of symbolism. The Papal jurisdiction does not cease on the death of a Pope, for it was conferred on the Church until the end of the world. Although the Great-Chamberlain cannot exercise jurisdiction, he keeps the emblems of it during the interregnum. The new Pope takes possession of them when he ascends the throne, and they disappear immediately from the arms of the Camerlengo. (*Plate 5; No. 21*).

These same signs – the keys and the pavilion – are used by the Sacred College of Cardinals, the Apostolic Chamber and by some pontifical institutes and seminaries. Moreover, some lay dignitaries of the Pontifical Court bore them as heraldic charges or

---

* In German known as "Basilikaschirm"; in French, "Ombrelle"; in Italian it is often called "Gonfalone" – presumably from its frequent use on gonfalons or ecclesiastical banners.

PLATE I

1. The armorial bearings of Pope Paul VI, Giovanni Battista Montini, b. September 26, 1897, elected Pope on June 26, 1963. The Montini family arms, known since the 16th century, were simplified and represented in a more modern style when he became Archbishop of Milan.

     Pope Paul VI died on 7 August 1978. The flag of the Papal Swiss Guard (Pl. VII) will now bear the arms of the new Pope.

PLATE II

2. The arms of John Joseph *Cardinal* Wright, who was Bishop of Pittsburgh before he was created Cardinal in 1969. Cardinal Wright was born in Dorchester, Archdiocese of Boston, July 18, 1909.

3. The arms of Count Paul de Huyn, *Patriarch* of Alexandria; b. 1868; Bishop of Brno 1904; Prince Archbishop of Prague and Primate of Bohemia 1916; Patriarch of Alexandria 1921; d. 1946. He was a Bailiff Gr. Cross of Justice of the Sovereign Military Order of Malta.

4. The arms of Michael George Bowen, *Archbishop* of Southwark since 1977; b. April 23, 1930 in Gibraltar.

5. The arms of Arthur Hughes, *Bishop* of Hieropolis since 1945; b. 1902 in London. Bishop Hughes was promoted Archbishop of Aprus and Internuncio to Egypt in 1947; d. 1949.

PLATE III

6. The arms of *Abbot Nullius* Catalan, O.S.B., (d. 1959) of New Norcia in Australia, third Abbot of the Benedictine Abbey of the Holy Trinity. For reasons of heraldic clarity the style and shield are here somewhat simplified.

7. The arms of *Abbot* Leodegar Hunkeler, OSB; b. 1887, d. 1956; Abbot of Engelberg, Switzerland, 1931-1956. The quarterings show: 1) the arms of Knight Conrad of Seldenbüren, founder of the Abbey, 2) the family arms of Abbot Leodegar Hunkeler, 3) the canting arms of the Abbey, being an angel on a mountain, 4) the arms of Habsburg, commemorating a fief the Abbey once held from the Emperor.

8. The arms of a *Prelate di Fiocchetto*, Prince Don Ugo Boncompagni-Ludivisi; b. 1856, d. 1935. He became a priest in 1895 after the death of his second wife and later Vice-Chamberlain (Camerlengo) of the Holy Roman Church.

9. The arms of Mgr. John Rast, *Protonotary Apostolic.*

2

RESONARE CHRISTVM

3

4

5

6

7

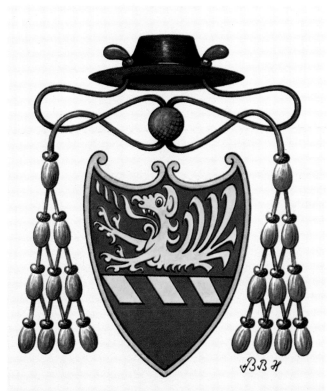

8

9

IV

10

11

12

13

14

BENEDICITE DOMINO

15

16

PRAEDICAMVS CRVCIFIXVM

17

PRAEDICAMVS CRVCIFIXVM

18

PRAEDICAMVS CRVCIFIXVM

PLATE IV

10. The arms of Mgr. O'Shea, *Prelate of Honour.*
11. The arms of Mgr. Giovanni Tonucci, *Chaplain to His Holiness.* Mgr. Tonucci was for two years Secretary at the Apostolic Delegation in London.
12. The arms of *Canon* O'Flynn.
13. The arms of Fr. Michael Scott Napier, Very Reverend Provost, *Superior* of Brompton Oratory, London. He is also a Chaplain of the Order of Malta.
14. The arms of Fr. Richard Frost, *Priest* of Arundel & Brighton Diocese, Catholic Chaplain at Sussex University, Brighton.
15. The arms of H. E. Fra Hubert (Marquess) Pallavicini, Bailiff Grand Cross of Justice of the Sovereign Military Order of Malta. He is a professed lay *Religious* with vows.
16. Here we have an example of how a prelate's achievement changes when he is promoted to a higher rank or to another See. Mgr. Julius Döpfner became Bishop of Würzburg in 1948 at the age of 35. The shield he then adopted is of no heraldic interest here. In 1957 he became *Bishop of Berlin.* The arms of Berlin Diocese are quartered and show in their quarterings the arms of four dioceses which existed within the territory covered by the present Diocese of Berlin, established in 1930, viz. Brandenburg, Havelberg, Cammin and Lebus. The shield of the diocese being quartered, the personal arms of Bishop Döpfner could only be placed in the centre, i.e. in pretence.
17. In 1958 Pope John XXIII created Bishop Döpfner *Cardinal* and the green bishop's hat had to be replaced by the red cardinal's hat.
18. In 1961 Cardinal Döpfner was promoted *Archbishop of Munich and Freising.* The episcopal cross had to be changed to the archiepiscopal double cross and the personal arms had to be quartered with the arms of the Archdiocese of Munich and Freising. Cardinal Döpfner died in 1976.

    The development of his arms makes it clear how absolutely wrong it it is to be rigid about how a bishop's arms should be composed in the shield with the diocesan arms, to affirm, for instance, that they must always be impaled. An artist with sufficient heraldic sense and knowledge will in every case choose the composition that gives the best heraldic result: i.e., that displays the given elements in the most harmonious way.

The Emperor Constantine presents Pope Sylvester with a tiara in AD 311 while a bishop carries the pavilion; from a 13th century fresco.

Pope Liberius (r.352-366) on his way to S. Maria Maggiore in Rome, with a monk carrying the pavilion.

ornaments. By ancient custom the pavilion belongs to all the Basilicas, of which it is the characteristic emblem. It is more richly adorned for the Major Basilicas than for the Minor. This umbrella can be seen in all the Basilicas of the world, and is also borne in processions.

In heraldry the Pavilion does not appear until the Fifteenth Century. As a charge (that is, as an heraldic figure on the shield) it is seen for the first time, with the keys, on a seal of Caesar Borgia, who in his way represented the temporal power of the Church at this period.

In composition with family arms, and even as external ornaments, the Pavilion and keys are also borne by families which have given a Pope to the Church, or by those to whom the Popes have conceded them as a privilege for services rendered to the Church.

The regulations of the Heraldic Council of the Kingdom of Italy (Consulta Araldica) required that the use of these emblems by the authorized families be preceded by a formal recognition by the heraldic commission of Rome. Each case had to be put forward and verified.

The Pavilion also appears among the manuscript illustrations of Matthew of Paris, mentioned before. Hauptmann expresses the opinion that this illustration shows an early form of tiara hoisted on a lance. He points out that the parading of military insignia on poles, in the fashion of the ancient Roman Army, was preserved into heraldic times. He believes that the tiara itself may have served in this way as a war-ensign and that, later, engravings representing it as such were misinterpreted.

Certain old paintings, a fresco of the Twelfth Century in the Church of the Quattro Coronati in Rome, for example, show a baldachin of the type used to receive illustrious persons such as kings and princes. At first this baldachin served as a parasol or umbrella to protect the visitors from sunshine and rain. Later it was used simply as a sign of honour and respect, and, forgetful of its original purpose, it was merely borne in front of the prince as an object required in the pomp of the reception.

This would explain why these Pavilions are to be found in the Basilicas and have become their distinctive signs. They had to be kept ready to receive the Sovereign Pontiff when he arrived for a ceremony.

Formerly, Papal Basilicas existed only in Rome. Since the last Century the privileges of a Basilica, amongst which is the right to possess a Pavilion, have been granted to many other famous churches.

4

THE MITRE

The sign, *par excellence,* of episcopal dignity is the mitre. It is a liturgical ornament. More than any other heraldic ensign it represents a sacred rank.

Although the mitre may appear at the same time on bishops, abbots and even canons, nonetheless it should be considered as a peculiarly pontifical prerogative, and strictly speaking only for bishops who are true "Pontifices". The other prelates, to whom the mitre is granted by privilege, only have pontifical rights *ad usum,* and not *ad exercitium* in the manner of bishops. In fact, the exercise of those sacred functions for which the liturgical laws prescribe the pontifical insignia is reserved exlusively to bishops.

Like the tiara, the mitre, or "infula", is a headgear whose name comes from antiquity. The shape has changed a great deal. In ancient Rome the "infula" was a priestly head-band, usually white, and was worn in the manner of a diadem, or turban, from which hung two ribbons. It was worn also by persons imploring the protection of the gods in the temples, and it was tied round the heads of sacrificial victims; a fact which bears witness to its primitive religious meaning.

The Latin word *mitra* denotes a banded bonnet, or else a kind of turban which in Rome was worn almost exclusively by women, though in the east men wore it as well. In Greek, equally, the word *mitra* means a band and a diadem.

Formerly Moses had prescribed a head-piece for the high priests. But our mitre has nothing in common with the *kideria (miznephet)* of the Old Testament.

The mitre cannot be found in Rome as a liturgical and pontifical head-gear before the Tenth Century; it

An Italian silver bust of a 17th century bishop wearing the Mitra Preciosa.

The arms of Mgr. Henri-Charles du Camboust de Coislin, Prince-Bishop of Metz, d.1732.

The arms of Dr. Ruben Josefsson, former Lutheran Archbishop of Uppsala and Primate of Sweden. His personal arms contain the rose from the arms of Martin Luther and are quartered with those of the Archdiocese.

is not impossible that it comes from the extra-liturgical hat of the Pope. It is hard to contest its relationship with the tiara. At first it was probably the same bonnet; diverse forms may gradually have been conceived for different purposes. Thus the mitre became the ensign of the bishop, and the tiara the princely ensign of the Popes.

There is no mention whatsoever in the Sacramentaries and Pontificals of the Ninth and Tenth Centuries of a liturgical head-dress. Even on Eleventh Century seals the bishops are depicted bare-headed. Mitres started to appear on seals from the Twelfth Century, with increasing frequency, beginning in England and in France.

Up to the pontificate of Leo IX (1049-1054), the mitre had been worn only in Rome by Popes and Cardinals. From that time it was conferred also on foreign bishops, one of the first to receive the distinction being Bishop Eberhard of Trier. This ornament quickly became an episcopal ensign after a number of bishops had received the mitre as a privilege of honour, and from then on bishops used it commonly and without special concession. The Popes accepted this usage tacitly, and perhaps they even wished to make it general, in order to establish a uniform discipline.

The mitre was granted to an abbot, for the first time, in 1063 under Alexander II. It was Abbot Engelsinus of St. Augustine's Monastery at Canterbury. Later, many abbots received it, either because they aimed at episcopal grandeur or because the Popes wished to honour monasteries and add to the solemnity of the divine service.

In a letter addressed to the Archbishop of Sens (towards 1126), St. Bernard of Clairvaux reprimands certain abbots who, by great effort and expense, procured the privilege of pontifical ornaments for themselves, and Peter of Blois expressed the same thought in a letter to his brother, Abbot William of Blois. The Church, however, continued to confer these privileges.

In 1266 Clement IV ordered abbots *nullius* to wear mitres embroidered with gold at councils and synods, but with no precious stones and gold leaf. Abbots not enjoying exemption, on the other hand, could only wear a simple white mitre. The bishops had had cause to complain about abbots who, instead of being satisfied with their extant privileges, dressed like bishops.

These limitations concerning the use of the abbot's mitre constitute, by corollary, approval of authorised usage. The Roman Pontifical, in fact, provides a ceremony for the blessing of an abbot, during the course of which the bishop takes from the altar the pontifical ornaments to hand them to the abbot whom he has just blessed.

The usage of the mitre by canons is even earlier than that of abbots, for in 1051 Leo IX granted the mitre to the *"cardinals"* (canons) of Besançon Cathedral.

At times the mitre, the crozier and other pontifical insignia were even granted to temporal princes by the Popes. The oldest example of such a privilege dates back to Nicholas II (1059-1061), who granted it to Duke Spytihnev of Bohemia. A little later Alexander II decorated Duke Vratislas with the Mitre, a favour which was confirmed in 1073 by Gregory VII. Roger of Sicily is supposed to have received it from Pope Lucius II (1144-1145) in addition to the crozier, ring, dalmatic and sandals. Innocent III, in his turn, gave it to Peter of Aragon in 1204.

The rite of Imperial Consecration included bestowing the mitre. The granting of the pontifical head-dress to temporal princes, as happened several times in the course of the Middle Ages, was the expression of the close relations existing between the temporal and spiritual powers, as, for example, between the Emperor and princes representing the temporal power, and the Pope, Vicar of Christ, as the personification of all spiritual power.

It happened later that even abbesses, like the Abbess of Conversano, near Bari, succeeded in acquiring a pectoral cross, ring, crozier and, sometimes, even a mitre.

This Abbess of Conversano, arrayed in pontifical ornaments, exacted the homage of the local clergy each year, and her behaviour earned her the title of The Monster of Apulia, for she even claimed canonical power over the clergy.

The history of the Church furnishes other examples in France, Germany and in Spain, where the Abbesses of Santa Maria de las Huelgas, near Burgos, were as solemnly vested as those of Conversano. Through the Bull *Sedis Apostolicae* in 1628, they succeeded in obtaining from Urban VIII the recognition of the wide ecclesiastical jurisdiction which they had exercised for

The arms of the Abbey of St. Benedict, Atchinson, Kansas, U.S.A.

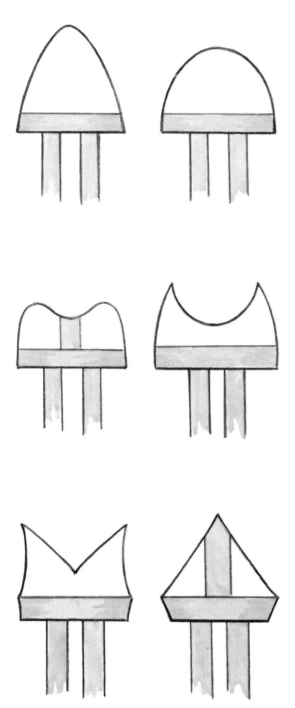

some centuries, and the title of Abbess *Nullius.* This state of things was not abolished until the Bull *Quam Diversa* of 12th July, 1873.

The Abbesses of Conversano were to witness an earlier limitation of their power. The clergy brought an action, on the 19th June, 1707, through the Sacred Congregation of bishops and regulars and forced the Abbess to change her ceremonial. The reception of feudal homage was simplified and the Abbess could no longer wear a mitre and carry a crozier; she could only place them on a table beside her. Enriched by the experience of past centuries, Canon 118 abolished such jurisdiction totally, once and for all.

The mitre has never belonged to abbots in their own right, nor to canons or any sort of prelate below the rank of bishop; *Ratione Dignitatis,* it is the prerogative of bishops alone. For all those prelates who are not bishops, it is a mere privilege. In the Bulls of concession its use always appears as a gracious favour of the Apostolic See. It is rarely granted without restriction of use and decoration for prelates who are not bishops. No one can make use of it without justifying his right to it, and those who have it by special privilege only, are obliged to hold strictly to the letter of the grant (D.2; D.3; D.11; n.5.).

Logically these limitations apply also to the armorial use of the mitre.

As already mentioned the mitre has undergone a whole series of transformations since its introduction in the liturgy. At the dawn of the Eleventh Century it was conical or hemispherical. Later it was divided from front to back. Since about 1125 it has been made up of two pointed pieces called horns, rising from each side and slightly inclined toward each other, held together by the lining. The Twelfth Century mitre no longer had the "horns" at the side, but fore the aft of the head. This evolution can be followed particularly well on the medieval seals.

At first the mitre was very short, rising vertically, and at the top the two horns bent in to a point. From the Fourteenth Century it grew in stature and size and was increasingly bejewelled and embroidered, even adorned with solid gold. The ornamentation became so exaggerated that eventually some mitres were of crushing weight. Some weighed fifteen pounds.

Liturgical law distinguishes, according to decoration, between three different kinds of mitre: the precious mitre, the golden mitre (*auriphrygiata*) and the white simple mitre. Without an established precedent, or specific mention in the grant, prelates below the rank of bishop are entitled only to the simple mitre.

The ground-colour of the mitre is now always white or gold. Hanging down from the back there are two *infulae* or ribbons, which are also white or gold with a red lining like the mitre itself. These prescriptions must be strictly observed in heraldry. Formerly other liturgical colours were used, and the author knows of an old portrait of a bishop wearing a blue mitre embroidered in gold.

As to the symbolic meaning of the mitre, Innocent III (1198-1216) tells us: "The mitre means the knowledge of the Old and New Testaments. The horns are the two Testaments; the infulae are the spirit and the letter . . ."

During the consecration ceremony of a bishop, in the former latin rite the consecrating bishop presented the mitre pronouncing these magnificent words:

"Imponimus Domine, capiti huius Antistitis et agonistae tui galeam munitionis et salutis quatenus decorata facie, et armato capite, cornibus utriusque Testamenti terribilis appareat adversariis veritatis; et, te ei largiente gratiam, impugnator eorum robustus existat . . ."

Soon after the adoption of arms by bishops and abbots, they ensigned their shields with mitres. Since it was their head-dress it is reasonable that it came to occupy the same position over the shield as the warrior's helmet.

It must not be overlooked that the privilege of wearing a mitre does not always carry with it the right to use it in heraldic achievements. Protonotaries Apostolic, for instance, may use the mitre in the liturgy, but are strictly forbidden to use it in their arms. (D.15, n.18). Certain chapters of canons who have the use of the mitre are also forbidden its heraldic use, whilst others are explicitly allowed it. (D.7., D.8., D.9., D.11. n.27., D.12. n.XXVII).

French and Italian bishops, from the outset, made much less use of the mitre in their heraldry than others.

Early seals show the development of the mitre; these portrait seals are from Tournai and the one overleaf is Finnish.

They preferred, as is now common use, to ensign their shield more simply with the ecclesiastical hat and cross. The decree concerning episcopal arms of Benedict XV (15th January 1915), does not mention the mitre (D.16), and since then its use in heraldry is generally going out of favour in the Roman Catholic Church, while the Church of England maintains the primitive usage. (*Plate 6; No. 26*).

5

THE CROZIER

The crozier, with the mitre, is pre-eminently important in heraldic art as an emblem of pontifical dignity. Like the sceptre it is a sign of jurisdiction, pointing the symbolism of the Good Shepherd. This meaning, however, is not exclusively implied; prelates without effective jurisdiction, such as titular bishops, have the right to carry it on suitable occasions; nonetheless several facts prove its fundamental meaning.

For example, the crozier is always laid down during prayer. A bishop may only carry it within his own diocese where he has jurisdiction. Outside his diocese a bishop should only use it with the consent of the local ordinary, or when authorized by the Holy See to perform ordinations or certain benedictions.* Abbots bear their crozier only within their monasteries, and outside of them under the conditions noted above.

An abbess may bear a crozier when processing or for certain official functions within the abbey, and adorn her arms with it; this, however, is only by way of exception. They may bear the crozier to recall some formerly exercised jurisdiction, but since in contemporary law they have no real ruling power outside their convent the crozier in their hands, or behind their shields, means nothing more than a certain motherly *potestas dominitiva ecclesiastica* concerning the government of their abbey.

The arms of the Diocese of Chur, Switzerland.

---

* Caeremoniale Episcoporum I, XVIII, 5.

Together with the pallium, the crozier is probably among the most ancient of ecclesiastical emblems. Commenting on the ancient *Ceremonial of Bishops* Catalano asserts that it had been considered an emblem of episcopal jurisdiction since the Fourth Century: Isidore of Seville (560-636) also speaks of the crozier as a symbol of the ruling power of bishops, but it is certain that some abbots have borne the crozier since the Seventh Century. At first it served as a pilgrim's staff or walking stick for the preachers of the Gospel sent out by the Church. Later the crozier became the characteristic sign of a high priest.

Originally these croziers were made of wood or iron, then precious metals came increasingly into favour. Hugh of St. Victor and Sicard of Cremona gave the following explanation of their form: *"curva trahit, recta regit, pars ultima pungit"* – that is – the hook serves to pull, the straight stick to lead, and the point to goad. The profound symbolism of the pastoral crozier is very concisely expressed in the following verse:

> *"Collige sustenta stimula*
> *vaga, morbida, lenta"**

that is – gather together the poor who wander about the world (*Collige vaga* for 'the hook'); raise the weak, the sick and sinners (*sustenta morbida* for 'the stem'); urge the slow, the lazy and the negligent (*stimula lenta* for 'the point'). There lies a programme of life for a pastor of souls!

In the latin rite of a bishop's consecration, the consecrating bishop used to say: *"Accipe baculum pastoralis officii; ut sis in corrigendis vitiis pie saviens, judicium sine ira tenens, in fovendis virtutibus auditorum animos demulcens, in tranquillitate severitatis censuram non deserens. Amen."*

As a symbol of jurisdiction, the crozier was one of the principal objects of the early disputes over Investitures. Granted the great importance given to symbols in the Middle Ages, for a temporal sovereign to hand over the insignia of spiritual dignity during the investiture of a bishop or abbot was regarded as the conferring of an ecclesiastical office by a layman, and the subordination of the spiritual to the temporal power. As history records,

---

* Pontificale Romano, vol. I. p. 459.

Veiled crozier of Abbot Frowin (r. 1142-1178) of Engelberg, Switzerland.

The arms of Dom H. de Sainte-Marie, Abbot of Clairveaux, Luxembourg. The veiled crozier appears between the arms of the Abbey and the Abbot.

.H. I

The arms of Dr. Mauritius Fürst, Abbot of Mariastein, Switzerland.

the struggle ended in the submission of the Emperor, who had to admit that the Church alone could confer its insignia, and possessed freedom to decide on the granting of ecclesiastical offices.

Popes do not carry a crozier. The explanation is given in a charming legend dating from the Xth Century. St. Thomas Aquinas tells it in a few words: "The Bishop of Rome does not have a crozier because Peter sent his to resuscitate one of his disciples. The latter retained the crozier and later became Bishop of Trier. To commemorate this incident the Pope carries the crozier in the diocese of Trier only, and never elsewhere – thus signifying that his power is without limit, since the hook marks a limitation of power" (IV Sent. XXIV, III, 8).

Even when cardinals had not been ordained bishops, they had a right to the mitre and crozier (canon 239 § 1, 13°); the same applies to abbots and prelates *nullius* (canon 325) and other abbots who have received the abbatial blessing (canon 625). Other prelates and dignitaries have these insignia only if granted by particular privilege.

To distinguish the bishop's crozier from that of abbots and other lesser prelates, the latters are provided with a veil (*velum*) which is attached to the node of the stem. This is a small silken cloth (*panisellus*) also called a *sudarium* (shroud), which prevented the often moist bare hand from coming into contact with the crozier; according to the Roman Rite gloves weer only worn by bishops.

It cannot be inferred from the original purpose of the veil that if abbots acquired the privilege of bishop's gloves, they could have *eo ipso* ceased from using the veil. The veil has become the distinctive sign of an abbot's crozier, particularly in heraldry, and even though most abbots receive the privilege of episcopal gloves, Rome for a long time insisted upon the veil.

However, today the rule concerning the veil is often broken. Indeed, Van Haeften notes that exempt abbots may leave off the *sudarium*, but he does not quote any source for this statement and it cannot be deduced from the documents on this question known to the author (D.2.; D.3.; D.4.; D.14.). On the contrary, the Benedictine Congregation of Monte Cassino was told that it had to conform to the decree of Alexander VII of 1659 (D.3.), which requires the veil on the Abbot's crozier. It is evidently impossible to invoke prescriptive right in the face of such explicit opposition by the competent authority.

There was another much discussed difference between bishops and abbots concerning the crozier, which could appear in their arms. It has been said that only bishops should carry the crozier with its crook turned towards the people. Abbots, on the contrary, were supposed to turn the crook inwards because they have jurisdiction only within the monastery. This distinction would have appeared in heraldry with the bishop's crozier turned outwards or towards the dexter of the shield, and the abbot's towards the sinister.

This custom was especially observed in France. The Count de Saint-Saud defends it against Mgr. Barbier de Montault, who claimed that bishops imposed this rule on abbots; in his estimation it was a matter of "puerility and vanity. . . that Rome has never approved and which time has treated as it deserves."

The Bishops' Ceremonial does indeed say that bishops should turn the crozier towards the people of their diocese. Nowhere is it laid down that this must find its expression in heraldry. As a rule such minutiae were disregarded, and in the classical period of heraldry such subtleties were unknown, an analogy being the shapes and positions of the helmet in lay heraldry which were introduced more recently.

In practice bishops' and abbots' arms, both ancient and modern, sometimes display the crozier now sinister, now dexter. We think that these differences were rather casual and that the crozier should be turned forwards, in heraldic terms to the dexter.

The arms of Dame Mary Caryll of Harting, elected Abbess of the English Benedictines (in exile) at Dunkerque in 1663.

6

THE PONTIFICAL HAT

The most commonly used external ecclesiastical ornament is the *Pontifical Hat*, also called the prelate's hat or, simply, the priest's hat. As we know headgear plays a major role in heraldry. It protects and adorns the head,

1420

the most noble part of the person, and is, at the same time, very conspicuous and easily recognized at a distance or in a crowd.

The original bearers of arms, the knights, quite naturally used their helmets and crests to mark their shields. The mitre, as the liturgical headgear of bishops, and very soon also the priest's hat, were used in the same way.

The first of the ecclessiastical hats to receive the distinction of a special tincture was the cardinal's hat. According to a universally accepted tradition, it was Innocent IV (1243-1254) who conferred the red hat on the cardinals at the time of the Council of Lyons, to have them recognized and distinguished from other prelates, especially during the great solemn cavalcades. The records of the Council do not, however, mention the introduction of the red hat. Most authors assume that it goes back to 1245.

The red hat is to remind the cardinals of their duty to defend the church even if it costs their blood and lives. It is, therefore, for them a form of exhortation; but we can note in passing that purple is also a princely colour *par excellence.*

In shape, the cardinal's hat was a pilgrim's hat with a wide brim. The brim is pierced with two cords ending in tassels. Formerly these cords were tied under the chin, or were brought together by a sliding ring in order to fix the hat.

Giving the red hat to the newly-elected cardinals in the public consistory, the Pope pronounced the following words:

"Ad laudem omnipotentis Dei et Sanctae Sedis Apostolicae Ornamentum accipe galerum rubrum, insigne singulare dignitatis cardinalitiae, per quod designatur, quod usque ad sanguinis effusionem inclusive, pro exultatione Sanctae Fidei, pace et quiete populi Christiani, augmento et statu Romanae Ecclesiae te intrepidum exhibere debeas. In nomine Patris et Filii et Spiritus Sancti.

Amen."

The hat which each cardinal received until recently long since lost the old classical shape. It was quite flat and very difficult to wear. Its only use was at the cardinal's funeral and after, when according to an age-old custom, it hung near his tomb. Pope Paul VI abolished the red hat and puts on the new Cardinals only a red cap.

The cardinal's hat made its appearance over the shield as an external mark at an early stage, either resting on the shield or a little above it. It can be seen in this way on the tomb of Cardinal Riccardo Petroni (d. 1313) in Siena Cathedral, and on the tomb of Cardinal Vias (d. 1328) at Avignon. The heraldic use of the cardinal's hat became widespread in the Fifteenth Century, and increasingly the mitre disappeared from the arms of cardinals.

At first there was no definite number of tassels at the end of the cords. Sometimes there were none at all. Hats can be seen with one, three, four or six tassels on each side and often the symmetry of the number is not observed. It was only in 1832 that the Sacred Congregation of Ceremonies decided to make the number of tassels uniform, fixing it definitively at fifteen on each side (D.13).

Following the cardinals, the Protonotaries Apostolic also adorned their shields with a hat; this hat was black, at least at first. The example was then followed by patriarchs, archbishops and bishops, especially in Italy. These prelates adopted a green hat as an ornament, which, according to Fox-Davies, originated in Spain where formerly the green hat was actually worn by the bishops. Moroni calls it a *semi-pontifical* hat and says that it was made of green silk, of the same shape as the cardinal's, and embellished with green cords and tassels. It is supposed to have been worn, with a processional cloak, on the occasion of solemn entry and cavalcades but not during sacred functions (that is, the prelates wore the hat arriving and departing). Today only the black hat is used almost exclusively, embellished with green cords and tassels as laid down by the ancient *Bishops' Ceremonial*. Thirty years ago the then Archbishop of Urbino wrote to the author to say that he still used an all-green hat according to the custom of his predecessors, but this was probably a unique instance, and its use confined to cathedral events of great solemnity.

Even if the colours of real and heraldic hats differed this would not be remarkable, for heraldry is not concerned with the real colour of objects adopted as emblems. The principles are not those of exact realism and faithful reproduction of nature. Lions, eagles and all other charges are painted in any of the heraldic tinctures or metals.

In spite of the freedom of choice in tinctures – a freedom which is normally strictly limited to the accepted heraldic colours, ecclesiastical heraldry admits purple for

The arms of Gordon Joseph Cardinal Gray, Archbishop of Edinburgh.

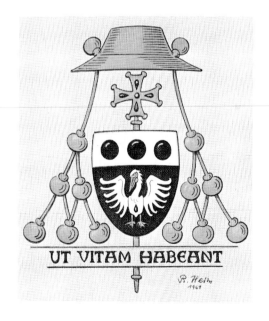

The arms of Mgr. Alfons Karl Kempf, Titular Bishop of Limyra.

69

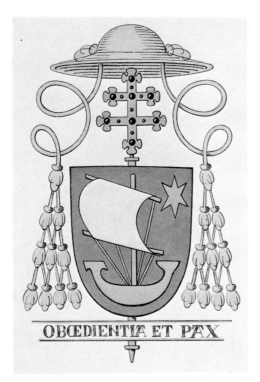

The arms of Archbishop Corrado Bafile, former Apostolic Nuncio in Germany, now a Cardinal.

The arms of Cardinal Carlos Carmelo de Vasconcellos Motta, former Archbishop of Sao Paolo, Brazil.

certain prelates' hats just because they are actually that colour. The cords and tassels of Protonotaries' and domestic prelates' full-dress hats were *rubini* and *violacei coloris*, and it seems that full hats in purple were once worn.

The later heraldry which introduced differing crowns to mark degrees of nobility did not shrink from using ecclesiastical hats to indicate hierarchical differences, and it has to be admitted that these hats offer all the advantages required for this purpose.

It was the Seventeenth Century heraldist, Pierre Palliot, who, having tried to establish a hierarchy of helmets and crowns, made one of the first attempts to systematise a similar usage for hats. He used as his source the manuscript of a certain Father Compain, whom he does not identify more fully. It is more than likely, however, that this is his contemporary, Father Matthieu Compain, S.J., rector at Chalon (d. 12th November, 1675 at Lyons.) In Jesuit schools where sons of the nobility were brought up the teaching of blazoning was held in high esteem. This could well explain how Father Compain came to prepare a manuscript on this subject. The same educational purposes spurred Father François-Claude Menestrier to enrich the literature of Heraldry with his many analytical and systematic works.

But it was not easy to bring clerical hats under uniform control until the *Motu Proprio* of Saint Pius X (D.15.), which laid down regulations for most of the lesser prelates whose customs were not well regulated. The few irregularities of usage which exist and persist among the ranks of green hats may be regarded as justified by their immemorial age.

7

THE PALLIUM

In more recent ecclesiastical heraldry the archbishop's pallium often appears above or below, or even on the shield. Heraldry has good reasons for making use of this emblem known already in the earliest years of Christianity.

A quite exceptional importance is attached to it. It is the symbol of very great powers, and only by the pallium can a residential be distinguished from a titular archbishop.

The Code of Canon Law deals with the pallium under six canons which are of interest to us, for the right to bear it carried with it the right to make use of it heraldically.

The pallium is above all a Papal liturgical ornament. It is the symbol of the Pope's supreme pastoral power, and indicates his task of shepherding and leading the faithful and their pastors. Derived from the Roman toga, it is nowadays a circular band of white wool, about two inches in width and adorned with black crosses; it is worn about the shoulders, and two similar bands about twelve inches long hang from it over the chest and back.

It is interesting to see the successive transformations of this vestment, which at first was a sort of wrap-around cloak which covered the other clothing. Later it was worn folded, and finally it was reduced to a narrow band. From being a major part of the consular costume it has become a simple symbolic ornament.

By the Fourth Century it already existed as a liturgical emblem of the Pope. Moreover, it had an ancestor in the *omophorion*, a similar ornament, used even earlier in the Eastern Church.

The bestowal of the pallium by the Pope on other metropolitans dates from the beginning of the Fourth Century. The obligation to solicit the Pope for it has been attested since the latter half of the Ninth Century. Before this period it was a simple distinction and only by way of exception were specific powers attached to it. Later it became an attribute of metropolitans indicating a degree of participation in the power of the Pope. Since the Eleventh Century reception of the pallium has been subject to an oath of fidelity to the Pope, and archiepiscopal power was bound to it in such a way that it could not be exercised until the pallium had been received – (Canon 276). Innocent III (1198-1216) forbade anyone to style themselves archbishop until they had received the pallium.

Since, in times past, one had to go in person to collect the pallium it often meant that some time elapsed before an archbishop could exercise his office. The resulting complications made this emblem increasingly an embarrassment. At present the Cardinal Proto-deacon is entrusted

Pope Paul VI wearing the pallium.

The arms of George Basil Cardinal Hume, Archbishop of Westminster. The family arms are impaled with those of the diocese (gules, a Pall proper surmounted by a fleur-de-lis argent) which are not officially approved because Catholic dioceses in England are not yet recognised as corporate bodies.

with the power of handing over the pallium to the new Archbishop or his proxy (Canon 239 § 3).

When bishops are, by special privilege, granted the pallium it does not confer any new powers, but is purely honorific. Metropolitans on the other hand are obliged to ask the Pope for the pallium, either in person or through a proxy, within three months of their consecration, or, if they were already bishops, beginning with their canonical appointment in Consistory (Canon 275). This same canon reminds recipients explicitly that the pallium signifies archiepiscopal power, a fact also expressed in the prelate's ritual request for the pallium: *Ego N. electus Ecclesiae N. instanter, instantius, instanissime peto mihi tradi et assignari Pallium de corpore Sancti Petri sumptum in quo est plenitudo pontificalis officii.*"

Metropolitans do not have the right to wear their pallium outside their own province. If an archbishop resigns he does not lose the pallium but no longer has occasion to wear it. Rome has never decided whether or not heraldic use of the ornament should be simultaneously dropped. As it had belonged to him nobody would deny him the right; however, with no cause to wear it and no archiepiscopal power any more, it seems logical to give it up. If a Metropolitan loses his pallium or is translated to another archdiocese, he must be granted another pallium (Canon 278), the reception of which is a condition for the exercise of his archiepiscopal power, as it was in the first place – (cf. Canon 276).

It is not permitted to lend, give or bequeath the pallium and each one received must be buried with the recipient – (Canon 279).

It is difficult to represent the pallium artistically in heraldy. From the Fifteenth Century it has often been shown in England within the shield of an archbishopric. This is the most aesthetically pleasing way to depict it, although thereby it ceases to be an external sign of dignity and becomes a charge.

To be a sign of dignity the pallium should stand outside the shield. Attempts have been made to put a small piece of it above the shield, (straight or slightly bent), bearing three black crosses. Others hang it above the shield in such a way that it drapes over the field of the shield. This may be convenient, but it is open to the objection that an external ornament should remain totally outside the shield and not encroach upon it. A further method of depicting the pallium is to put it under the lower part of the shield, alowing it to show at the bottom of the latter, in the manner of the ribbons proper to orders of knighthood in secular heraldry. In this case it covers the shaft of the cross and the whole achievement looks too long. Undoubtedly the British custom of placing it as a charge within an Archbishop's shield offers the best solution to this problem of heraldic art.

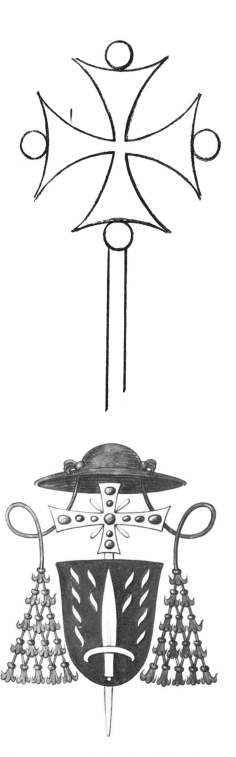

8

THE CROSS

The cross displayed by patriarchs and archbishops since the Fourteenth Century, first in the shield, and then somewhat awkwardly in front of it, and finally in pale behind the shield, (later adopted by bishops as well), is mentioned in the *Roman Pontifical* as an heraldic external ornament. It has nothing to do with a bishop's pectoral cross, but is the cross mentioned in Canon 274, 6°, which is carried in procession before the Pope, his legates, the patriarchs and archbishops. It must not, however, be confused with the usual cross carried at the head of lesser ecclesiastical processions. The shape of these crosses may be identical, but their significance is radically different. The cross carried before the Pope, his legates, patriarchs, and archbishops, belongs to their hierarchical character and must precede them immediately; nobody can come between them and the cross. The other cross simply marks the religious character of the procession.

The cross which has been carried before the Pope since the Fifth Century has always had a single transverse bar. This custom was soon adopted by the papal legates because they represent the person of the Pope. In 1215 Innocent III allowed patriarchs to have the cross carried before them everywhere except in Rome, or places where the Pope or his legate, bearing the insignia of apostolic dignity, were present. Clement V (1305-1314) extended this right to archbishops, even outside their own dioceses.

The Bishops' Ceremonial does not allow this cross to

The arms of Cardinal Willebrands, now Archbishop of Utrecht. When he became a Cardinal he was Titular Bishop of Mauriana; hence the simple cross in his achievement.

73

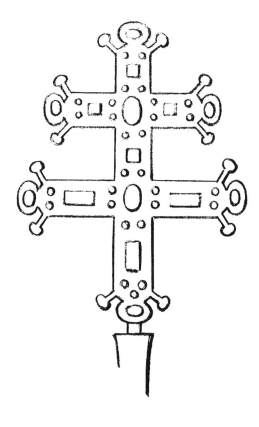

them : on the contrary it says explicitly : *"si vero celebrans fuerit Archiepiscopus, aut Archiepiscopo major, aut habens privilegium, ut crux ante se deferatur archiepiscopalis. . . ."* Therefore it is obviously an archiepiscopal emblem.

However, bishops make use of this cross in heraldry, and it is universally recognized in the Roman Catholic Church as an emblem of episcopal rank. It is even the one heraldic emblem that only bishops have the right to bear. Cardinals who were not consecrated bishops did not use it. Nowadays, when even cardinal deacons are bishops, they should, logically bear the emblem.

Let it be noted, however, that this cross does not form part of the papal heraldic achievement. The processional cross, according to liturgical law, is always simple (i.e. with one cross-piece), even when carried before the Pope. In heraldry patriarchs and archbishops first used the simple cross, but by the Fifteenth Century patriarchs adopted the double cross with two bars, the upper cross piece being the panel of the inscription that Pontius Pilate had put on the cross of Jesus. Since the Seventeenth Century many primates have done likewise, and now archbishops have assumed the heraldic use of the double traversed cross, largely because bishops had adopted the simple cross as an external ornament in heraldry, although they are still denied the personal right to have it carried before them in processions.

Today patriarchs, metropolitans and archbishops (including the titulars), adorn their arms with a double traversed cross and bishops use the simple cross. The triple traversed cross has occasionally appeared as a papal emblem, but purely as a result of the artists' ignorance for it has never been a formal papal device or emblem.

9

THE PRIOR'S STAFF

The arms of Archbishop Filippo Bernardini, former Apostolic Nuncio to Switzerland; the cross is that of the Order of the Holy Sepulchre.

The prior's or cantor's staff is a less important sign of dignity and is used less frequently. Like the crozier its origin can be traced to the pilgrim's staff, and in the course of time it has undergone artistic evolution. It is often made of silver, or of wood encased in finely chased silver. The upper part terminates with a knob in the form of an apple, a fleur-de-lys or a little house or chapel.

The staff is the emblem of certain chapter officials who do not have any right to pontifical insignia, such as provosts, priors, precentors or first cantors. The staff is used to give directions during the choir ceremonies, and was similarly used by priors and local superiors of certain monastic orders.

The general rule which we have met before can be applied in this case : the man who actually carries the staff is the one who has the right to use it as an heraldic ornament. The staff was mentioned by Bernard du Rosier who says that regular provosts, major priors of monasteries, administrators of cathedrals and collegiate churches bear it either during the solemnities of divine service or as an armorial ornament, it being a straight pastoral staff, not curved like that of abbots and bishops. At present it is little used in heraldry, but will be found in ancient achievements.

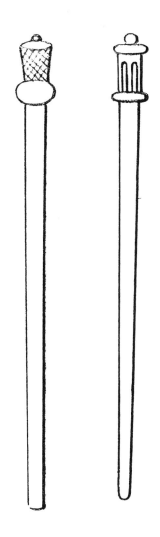

10

THE ROSARY

The rosary or chaplet is the heraldic sign of a religious. In particular it is used by those religious who have no right to other ornaments, i.e. who are not priests.

To mark their arms they surround their shields very simply with a rosary – nearly always a black one – made up of five decades of beads, the decades separated from each other by a bigger bead.

In heraldry it has figured occasionally in arms of superiors with the right to a staff, and is then represented in conjunction with the latter.

Female religious may use a lozenge or oval-shaped shield, proper to feminine heraldry, surrounding it with a rosary as a mark of their religious profession : abbesses may combine it with a crozier.

The ex-libris of the Rt. Hon. Viscount Monckton of Brenchley with the Chief of Religion and insignia of a Bailiff Grand Cross of the Order of Malta.

The ex-libris of D. C. R. Pehrson, Knight of Malta and Knight Officer of the Savoyard Order of SS Maurice and Lazarus.

Professed knights of the Sovereign Military Order of St. John of Jerusalem, who are religious, surround their shields with a silver rosary placed on and interlaced with the Maltese Cross. Their rosary has a small Maltese Cross at the bottom. (*Plate 4; No. 15.*)

11

THE DECORATIONS

As has just been said, members of certain Orders place their shields on a cross. This particularly concerns the two major surviving ancient Orders of Knighthood, the heraldic use of whose crosses was permitted to cardinals and bishops, who are forbidden the use of any other worldly decorations and orders of merit. (D.1. and D.16.)

The Order of St. John of Jerusalem, known as the *Order of Malta,* and the *Order of the Holy Sepulchre* have distinctive crosses which are well known in heraldry.

a) *The Maltese Cross,* or Cross of St. John, is an eight-pointed white cross whose points, it is said, represent the eight beatitudes. This Order, whose historical origins still are somehow in the haze of antiquity, is the most famous of the religious and military Orders to date from the crusades. By the Eleventh Century it was remarkably active as an Order of hospitallers, and had distinguished itself in glorious feats of arms, receiving a Papal charter in 1113 from Pope Paschal II. Evacuated from the Holy Land in 1310 it wrested the Island of Rhodes from the hands of pirates and retained it until 1522 as a sovereign principality. In 1530 it received the Island of Malta, together with two other territories, as a fief from the hands of the Emperor Charles V, and it was then that it became known as the ORDER OF MALTA. The sovereignty of the Order was preserved after the surrender of Malta to Napoleon in 1798, and although it no longer possesses any sovereign territory, it is still widely recognised as Sovereign in the international sphere and has its diplomatic representatives in many countries.

Clerics who belong to the Order, even if not professed, have often ornamented their arms with the emblems of the Order. They placed their shields on the Cross of Malta and, if they had a rank in the Order conferring the right, they added to their own charges those of the Order (Gules, a cross Argent) in chief,* the whole surrounded by a white rosary, if they had made profession. The author has often noted this custom, and Woodward makes comment on it. (*Plate 2, No. 3.*)

The rights of Cardinal bailiffs in this respect were confirmed by His Most Eminent Highness the Prince Grand Master of the Order some fifty years ago, and strictly the only others to enjoy these privileges are the professed members; all others should simply place their cross and ribbon at the bottom of the shield.

If this does not look aesthetically pleasing with some achievements then, in the writer's view, as heraldic art permits of great freedom in the interest of creating beauty, the plain Cross of the Order may be placed near the shield, wheresoever it looks best. Thus elegance is achieved, affiliation to the Order denoted, and heraldic pedantry avoided.

The Prince Grand Master quarters his family arms with those of the Order, the shield being on the eight-pointed cross and surrounded by a rosary; the whole is borne on a black princely mantle ensigned by the crown of rank. (*Plate 6; No. 25.*)

---

b) The second equestrian Order to have its cross used in ecclesiastical heraldry is the *Order of the HOLY SEPULCHRE*, whose emblem is the Cross of Jerusalem. This is a cross potent cantoned with four crosslets, the whole Gules.

This Order also dates back to the Crusades – albeit subject to lapse and revival – and has origins reputedly related to the conferment of Knighthood in the Church of the Holy Sepulchre in Jerusalem with the sword of Geoffrey de Bouillon. It received papal recognition in 1113 by Pope Pascal II and was restored by Pope Alexander VI in 1496.

Members of the Order of the Holy Sepulchre may place their shield on the cross of Jerusalem, which then appears behind the shield, or they may have it hanging on a black

The ex-libris of Professor Géza Grosschmid as a Knight of Magistral Grace of the Order of Malta.

The arms of Major Ronald Kinsey, T.D., O.St.J., J.P., F.S.A., Knight of the Order of the Holy Sepulchre.

---

* The baliffs Gr. Cross are also allowed to use the chief of the Order.

77

The arms of Dr. Joseph K. von Castelberg, Knight Commander of the Order of the Holy Sepulchre.

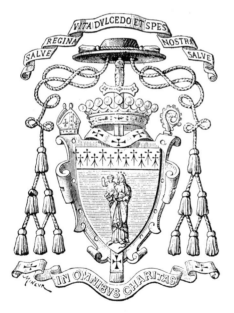

The arms of Mgr. Guillois, former Bishop of Puy and Count of Gap and of Velay. He used the temporal sword, instead of the cross, and a Count's crown. Such achievements are no longer tolerated.

ribbon below their shield, or, finally they may put the cross somewhere near their achievement, where it looks best, just to indicate their membership.

High dignitaries of the Order quarter the cross of Jerusalem with their personal arms.

In addition to the crosses of these equestrian orders, the cross flory of the *Dominican Order* can be found in ecclesiastical heraldry behind the shield of that Order's dignitaries and even ordinary members. It is also called the Dominican Cross and was probably at one time the sign of the Inquisition.

12

THE CROWNS

Prince-bishops and abbots often placed their arms on a mantle Gules lined with ermine, raised on both sides by cords or and ensigned by a prince's crown. Prelates whose sees preserved the princely title still used these ornaments until some 25 years ago. Many of them, however, had long since renounced the title as privileges relating to such principalities had been abrogated since the French Revolution, except in the Austro-Hungarian Monarchy.

If a see retained a nobiliary title the Church did not, until recently, forbid use of the corresponding emblems as exterior ornaments to its arms (D.16.). The same applied to those chapters of canons which possessed the title of count or baron for all their members.

Yet, in their official arms, the clergy should never make use of crowns which indicate hereditary and family nobility (D.1., D.16.). Priestly dignity is considered a higher state than that of nobility. That is why in certain slavonic languages the faithful address a priest with a title resembling that of a prince, according to ancient custom. Even the title *Don* (*Dominus*) commonly used in Italy is shared with princes and the oldest nobility in that country.

Moreover, the clergy have their own hierarchy and their own heraldic insignia. It would be regrettable if that order were disturbed by distinctions foreign to it. Clergy are all brothers and it should make no difference if they come from a powerful and famous or a poor and unknown family.

It is common enough to see crowns on the arms of ecclesiastical communities, congregations, monasteries, and confraternities. Doubtless their members would be moderately embarrassed if called upon to explain their meaning and source. It is difficult, indeed, suitably to difference corporate arms. Apart from the mural crowns proper to cities, there exists no heraldic sign capable of distinguishing corporations as such. When applied to corporate bodies, crowns in general nowadays have but a purely decorative purpose.

The arms of the Abbot Nullius of Einsiedeln in Switzerland. They were Princes of the Holy Roman Empire and used until recently the temporal sword in their achievements.

13

THE TEMPORAL SWORD

In days of old, as we know, the princes of the Church often made use of the honorific emblems and insignia of secular heraldry. Thus their arms could not readily be distinguished from those of the nobility. This custom, which with good reason seems to smack of pretension these days, has now fallen into complete desuetude. Naturally, clerics may have representations of arms traditional to their families in their own homes, but official ecclesiastical arms may not bear worldly attributes.

Among the secular emblems at one time allowed to adorn ecclesiastical arms was the temporal sword. It was by no means rare for bishops, abbots and even abbesses to bear a sword, placed in saltire with the crozier, or alone in pale behind the shield. This was the so-called temporal sword which indicated the power of capital punishment, namely the high justice granted to prelates in their territories by the temporal sovereigns.

The sword behind their shields was the symbol of this power. Since the secularisation of ecclesiastical principalities this custom has ceased entirely and the sword has disappeared from ecclesiastical arms; no regret need be felt at its passing.

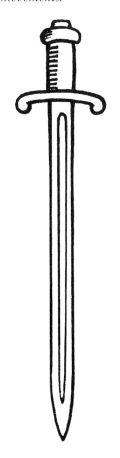

79

The arms of Mgr. Josef Stangl, Bishop of Würzburg, Germany.

It is widespread custom to put a motto under the shield. It is often held, wrongly, by those who know little about heraldry, that the motto is indispensable; yet it is an addition which does not properly belong to the armorial bearings themselves. The motto expresses in brief an ideal, a plan of life, and often more explicitly than the armorial bearings, it manifests the mentality of the man who chose it. It is, thus, not totally unconnected with the coat of arms, which also reveals something of the character and personality of its original bearer. Originally it might have been a war-cry.

There is often no apparent connection between the arms and the motto; nevertheless a certain parallelism can sometimes be discerned between them: both are distinctive marks of a person or a family; both pledge the honour of those who bear and glory in them; both may be of martial origin. At first both were meant to be a stimulus to courage in combat, then in all of life, and an encouragement to conduct oneself always with rectitude and generosity.

Prelates are fond of adopting concise quotations from Holy Scripture, but too frequently utilise pious sayings which are prosaic, insipid and devoid of originality.

The motto should sound well, be pithy and, if possible, ingenious and concise (not more than three or four words). Popular opinion often has it that the motto must, of necessity, relate to the devices of the arms. This is mistaken. If the design of the arms does not lend itself to a delicate and ingenious allusion, it is better not to distort the meaning of otherwise appropriate words to give them surface relevance.

The motto is inscribed legibly in capitals on a scroll if suitable of the same tincture as the shield. It can also simply be put below the achievement; this avoids complicating the design with scrolls, which are too often clumsy and graceless.

15

THE SUPPORTERS

In heraldic art it is not uncommon to find angels, human figures, animals, and even trees and pieces of architecture used as supporters, props and stays. The exterior ornaments of the shield may be ancient, but their origin is not exactly heraldic. They are decorative pieces. There was no place for supporters in knightly armour. They are show-pieces for display, often devised to fill up empty spaces and balance designs. They found their first application on seals dating from the end of the Twelfth Century.

Supporters, originally, were thus not essential elements of an achievement but pompous ornaments with which priests should not overcharge their arms, both from the ecclesiastical and the simple heraldic point of view, in spite of what may have been done in the past.

If the shield of a monastery is supported by an angel or saint, there can be no criticism; but a shield ornamented by a hat and pontifical insignia, and surrounded by animals, could not fail to seem a trifle odd. In any case, the official arms of a prelate do not have supporters.

For private use, on a bookplate for instance, it might be pleasant and allowed to represent ones patron saint together with ones shield.

The arms of Mgr. Leonard Weber, D.D. who died in 1969. The Prelate's Patron Saint, St. Leonard, patron of captives (lock and chain) and protector of horses, supports the shield.

The arms of Pope Gregory XV (Ludovisi, 1621-23), showing the Apostles Peter and Paul as supporters. Rules about not using Apostles were not always observed by engravers.

The ex-libris of Father Hermes Turwitt. His patron saint is Bishop Hugo of Grenoble, whose badge is the swan.

CHAPTER FOUR

I

THE ACQUISITION AND LOSS OF ECCLESIASTICAL ARMORIAL INSIGNIA

The principles which govern the acquisition, transmission and loss of armorial bearings are the basis of heraldic law. There are two matters to be distinguished in secular heraldic law; the acqustion and loss of the right to bear arms in general, and the acquisition and loss of a particular coat of arms and badges of rank.

As we have already had occasion to say, the right to bear any sign whatever is a natural human right. It is not limited to any privileged class; but, nevertheless, there are certain conventional signs which by common agreement are reserved for a certain status, certain ranks or certain public offices. Their use is an assertion which should, of course, correspond to reality.

The use of arms by clerics as private persons has never been the concern of the Church. That belongs to their personal rights prior to entering the clerical state. To repeat, the object of the heraldic law of the Church is not the shield and what it contains, but only those devices added outside the shield indicating the various ecclesiastical dignities.

In the first heraldic law promulgated by the Holy See, in 1644, Innocent X explicitly does not touch upon what is contained within the shield of the family arms of each individual. Benedict XV confirms this intention of the Church not to touch the personal arms of a cleric (D.16.).

The ecclesiastical heraldic legislation touches only the ecclesiastical element; that is, it gives the right to add ecclesiastical emblems of dignity to the achievement.

As noted earlier, the rules established by liturgical and ceremonial prescriptions apply equally in matters of

Pope Paul VI is crowned with the tiara presented to him by the Catholics of his former Archdiocese of Milan.

ecclesiastical heraldic law. This is a statement of fundamental importance.

Like ecclesiastical dress and liturgical ornaments and insignia, an ecclesiastical achievement is a matter of clerical privilege. The external ornaments, which characterize ecclesiastical heraldry, depend entirely on the rank held in the Church, whether it concerns a rank in the jurisdictional hierarchy, in which one is incorporated by canonical mission, or a rank in the hierarchy of order to which one is elevated by holy orders (Canon 109), or, finally, the hierarchy of honour which has been established by ecclesiastical authority.

It is of the nature of ecclesiastical insignia to be neither hereditary, nor transmissible by private contract. In the Roman Catholic Church ecclesiastical offices and dignities, of which liturgical and heraldic insignia are the symbols, can be conferred only by ecclesiastical authority. Everyone, without exception, must acquire them in person on entering the clerical state and by progressing up the ladder of the hierarchy.

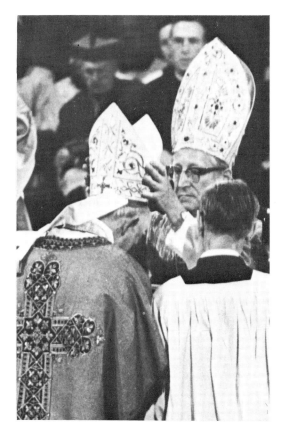

Archbishop Basil Hume, O.S.B., receives the mitre from the Apostolic Delegate during his consecration as Archbishop of Westminster.

1

THE ACQUISITION OF MARKS OF DIGNITY

The first condition of the right to bear ecclesiastical arms is obviously entry into the clerical status.

Since there are no heraldic signs to designate the degrees of the minor orders, and since access to hierarchical dignities presupposes the priesthood, it is necessary to be at least a priest to bear ecclesiastical arms except, however, in the case of some lay religious, a matter which will not be developed here in depth, although a few comments are pertinent.

Lay religious are seldom in a position to bear official arms in the Church. If they attain a position as superiors (having by custom coats of arms, like abbesses), their right to insignia is founded on their canonical institution. In any case, we are dealing here with basic principles, and not yet with the question of direct authorization to bear official arms.

Dom Egidio Gavazzi, O.S.B., receives the crozier from Pope Paul VI as a mark of dignity as abbot.

Of all the impediments to holy orders, that of illegitimate birth was of particular importance, partly owing to the difficulties raised in this matter by secular heraldic law, partly because of the canonical consequences thereby entailed. Illegitimate birth limits the capacity to bear arms, and despite any dispensation obtained with the priesthood in view it ultimately bars access to certain ranks of the hierarchy (Canon 991 § 3).

The treatment of illegitimate offspring in civil law has been variously nuanced in differing times and places. All possible permutations are known, including the giving of titles of nobility, the right to use the paternal name, the right to bear familial arms, total deprivation of all these; and inheritance with full rights. At times "bastard" was even an honorary title. After the Fifteenth Century, however, a bastard's arms were often differenced, two examples being the canton on a plain field and the bendlet sinister.

The ancient German view, which gave a degrading character to illegitimate birth, regrettably crept into ecclesiastical law during the Tenth and Eleventh Centuries. In civil law illegitimates were tainted injustly with disgrace, and in recruiting clergy the Church took account of this state of affairs while disapproving of such harshness. If the Church grants a dispensation, whether because of legitimation on the grounds of a subsequent marriage (Canon 1116), or by retroactive decree (*sanatio in radice,* Canon 1113), or, lastly, if the irregularity is extinguished as a consequence of solemn vows (Canon 984, 1°), the dispensed person obtains free access to holy orders and may receive non-consistorial benefices. (Canon 991, § 3), and such a status automatically brings with it the right to certain ecclesiastical armorial insignia. But without new special dispensations, illegitimates can become neither a cardinal (Canon 232, § 2, 1°) nor a bishop (Canon 331, § 1, 1°) nor an abbot or prelate nullius (Canon 320, § 2), nor a major superior of a religious congregation (Canon 504). The ecclesiastical capability of bearing arms is thus limited, depending as it does on the actual possession of the relevant dignity and office.

There is no way of achieving certain ecclesiastical dignities except by holy orders. This is the case with the priesthood and the episcopacy; the minor orders have

84

no heraldic insignia and are passed through rapidly on the way to the priesthood.

Other dignities (offices and benefices) can be obtained by canonical provision, which is the granting of an ecclesiastical office by the competent church authority according to the rules of Canon Law (Canon 147).

Because of the numerous requirements of Canon Law concerning ecclesiastical offices it follows that the heraldic law of the Church is much more severe in its regulation than nobiliary law. Ecclesiastical heraldry does not exist for the individual's benefit. Its aim is the distinction of the hierarchy on the grounds of function, and clerics occupy their offices not for themselves, but at the behest of the Church for the benefit and good of the faithful. Although the right to bear arms has nothing to do in general with belonging to a particular class, the right to bear the insignia of ecclesiastical rank depends exclusively on an individual's ecclesiastical status. No one may claim such a right by virtue of birth; ecclesiastical authority bestows it when granting the relevant office in the Church.

The conferring of ecclesiastical offices is regulated by special legislation which also implicitly governs the right to the corresponding signs of rank. (See Plate 4; Nos. 16, 17 and 18. Elevation from Bishop to Bishop *and* Cardinal to *Archbishop* and Cardinal).

The fact that the offices may be prebendal or non-prebendal has no bearing on heraldic law. Even if it is a matter of purely honorary office, the heraldic insignia are the same, for armorial usage is bound to the rank, and in no way to any possible income. Thus we may well dismiss the erroneous opinion of some authors that a simple priest needs to be in possession of a benefice before he can ornament his shield with an ecclesiastical hat.

In the matter of honorary titles or offices, nomination takes the place of canonical provision. The individual is designated and instituted by nomination and has no need to take possession in person.

Lord Monckton, (right), President of the British Association of the Order of Malta, investing a Knight with the Cross of Merit of the Order.

85

2

THE LIMITATION, DIMINUTION
AND LOSS OF MARKS OF DIGNITY

Our study must now deal with the three following questions:

> What juridical impediments are there to the acquisition of higher insignia?
>
> How can a cleric be deprived of certain insignia?
>
> When does he lose the right to all ecclesiastical insignia?

These three questions are closely linked, for the same causes can lead to the loss of some or all insignia. These causes are: the regular loss of office; the loss of office as a canonical punishment; other more serious canonical punishments.

Insignia belong to an official as soon and as long as he legitimately occupies his position; that is *durante munere*. This rule is explicitly laid down in the case of vicars apostolic and prefects apostolic, who are not bishops (Canon 302), for apostolic administrators (Canon 315, § 2, 2°), for vicars-general (Canon 370, § 2), and for vicars-capitular (Canon 439; D.15. Nos. 62 and 76).

In certain religious orders, it is customary for the major superiors, when their office is at the end of its term, to continue to bear the title (Canon 515). If their constitutions allow the use of these titles, they may, as a consequence, also continue to bear the corresponding heraldic external ornaments.

1) *Loss of Office*

Loss of an ecclesiastical office is followed merely by the loss of the signs proper to such office, unless it be a question of punishment for crime and this punishment be combined with other ecclesiastical penalties.

There are many causes of loss of ecclesiastical office, and various effects in heraldic law are attached to these causes:

a) All offices naturally cease upon the death of the holder. After his decease his arms (together with the ornaments to which he was entitled at the time of death) are no longer used, except to decorate his tomb or other places which invoke his memory.

86

b) If a competent superior accepts, one may resign an office. (Canon 183, § 1).

In this case an office connected with jurisdiction must be considered separately from the holy orders (priestly or episcopal).

An office in the jurisdictional hierarchy may be withdrawn with all its accompanying privileges. A retiring official, however, keeps all the rights acquired by virtue of his ordination. The priesthood and the episcopacy impress an indelible character on the individual, and for this reason they cannot be lost like other functions; one can cease to exercise them publicly, without losing the corresponding privileges. This loss can only occur through degradation and reduction to the lay estate.

c) Loss of an office can also be the result of a legal regulation or the order of a competent superior (Canon 192, § 1.). In this case, personal fault may or may not be involved, and the loss of office may or may not have the character of a punishment.

d) Many ecclesiastical offices have a limited term, and the date of expiry is determined from the moment of appointment (Canon 183 § 1), or fixed by constitution, as in many religious congregations (Canon 505). In the same way, as before, the right to make use of official heraldic insignia is withdrawn when the office is relinquished, unless the title is retained *honoris causa* (Canon 515).

2) *Ecclesiastical penalties*

Whilst the mere loss of office entails, at most, a lessening of the right to certain signs of dignity, ecclesiastical penalties may impede any new promotion or even entail the total loss of ecclesiastical arms. The following penalties are involved :

a) *Excommunication* – The foremost among censures inflicted by Canon Law is that of excommunication. The excommunicated person is excluded from the community of the faithful (Canon 2257, § 1). He is not allowed to exercise any function or enjoy any ecclesiastical privilege (Canon 2263). He is not deprived of rank or ecclesiastical status. The armorial insignia are, therefore, not taken from him formally, but he cannot use them during the time that the excommunication lasts.

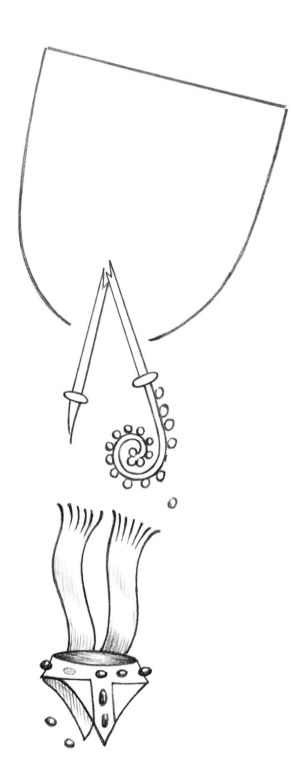

The excommunicate can no longer obtain any new offices or dignities, and he is not admitted to ordination (Canon 2265, § 1, 2° and 3°). This situation entails an impediment to any future promotion within the hierarchy, and consequently a limitation in the capability to bear ecclesiastical arms.

If the excommunicated person is publicly declared *vitandus* (to be avoided), he is then also deprived of office, dignity, prebend and any function at all (Canon 2266). He, therefore, loses any right to bear ecclesiastical insignia or marks of dignity.

b) *Interdiction* – Interdiction does not exclude one from the community of the Church. It is only the penal retention of certain spiritual benefits (Canon 2268, § 1). Places may come under interdict, in which case the people are affected only indirectly. If individuals are put under interdict the penalty affects them wherever they go. The person under interdict can obtain neither office nor dignity, and is excluded from ordination (Canon 2275, 3°). Personal interdiction, therefore, renders any ascent in the hierarchy impossible and limits the capability to bear ecclesiastical arms.

c) *Suspension* – This last ecclesiastical censure forbids the exercise of office or enjoyment of benefice (Canon 2278, § 1.). Suspended priests keep their heraldic rights, but these rights are limited as under excommunication or interdict (Canon 2283).

d) *Demotion* – Among the twelve 'vindictive penalties' for clerics (Canon 2298), certain of them entail more serious consequences, as far as heraldic law is concerned, than the corrective penalties. Thus, the third of these special penalties is the transfer to an inferior position, which causes a loss of the insignia attached to the higher office formerly occupied.

e) *Exclusion from Dignities* – The fifth of the twelve vindictive penalties reserved for clerics makes them ineligible for some or all dignities; the consequence of this situation is limitation to the insignia of those dignities and offices which remain accessible to them.

f) *Punitive Privation of Office* – The sixth of the penalties enumerated in Canon 2298, is the withdrawal of a benefice or office, the logical corollary of which is the loss of corresponding insignia.

g) *Privation of Ecclesiastical Dress* (Unfrocking) – The ninth and eleventh of the penalties mentioned in the same Canon is the temporary or perpetual privation of ecclesiastical dress, causing the loss of all insignia. Alluded to here is the everyday clerical dress, which distinguishes the cleric from the layman, but *a fortiori* this penalty includes liturgical ornaments and vestments, and, consequently, of all ecclesiastical heraldic insignia.

h) *Deposition* – The tenth of the vindictive penalties is deposition, entailing suspension from office and ineligibility for all ecclesiastical offices, dignities and benefices. The obligations and privileges of the clerical state, however, remain untouched by deposition (Canon 2303, § 1). Consequently all higher insignia are lost; ordinary ecclesiastical dress is left, and the simple priest's hat remains as an ornament.

i) *Degradation* – The last and most serious vindictive penalty for a cleric who has done wrong is degradation, which includes deposition, perpetual deprivation of clerical dress and reduction to the lay state (Canon 2305, § 1). The loss of all privileges naturally includes the loss of all heraldic rights.

The old Roman Pontifical contains a special ceremony for ritual degradation. The guilty man has to present himself, arrayed in all the ornaments of his dignity, and the officiating prelate strips him of them while uttering severe reprimands. Obviously it is difficult to persuade a guilty man to attend so humiliating a ceremony willingly, but the rite of deposition shows the concomitant losses in dramatic manner.

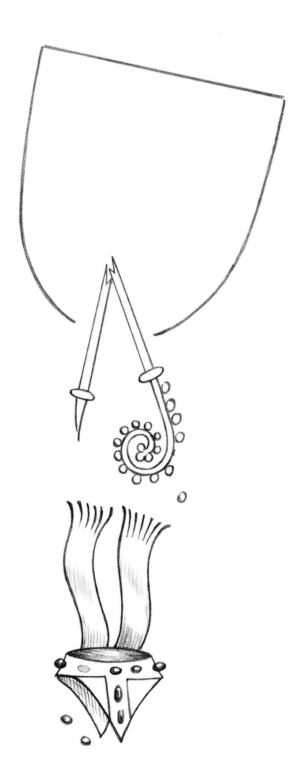

89

II

THE APPLICATION OF THE MENTIONED PRINCIPLES TO ALL RANKS OF THE HIERARCHY

It will now be demonstrated how the heraldic and juridical principles apply in practice to all the grades of the hierarchy.

THE POPE – The right to bear papal insignia (the tiara and keys) is acquired by acceptance of lawful election, for it is in accepting that the elected becomes a pope (Canon 109), and by divine right he immediately possesses in all its fulness the power of the primacy (Canon 219), symbolically represented by the well-known heraldic insignia. (Plate 1; No. 1).

It is logical enough that the exterior signs of office belong *ipso facto* to the *Supreme Pontiff* as soon as he possesses its prerogatives. Moreover, we know from the matter of canonical provision, that when an election requires no confirmation, its mere acceptance by the elected man immediately confers on him its full powers (Canon 176, § 2). The ceremony of coronation adds nothing. It is merely the first opportunity for the new pontiff to wear the tiara.

The right to bear ecclesiastical heraldic insignia is more closely connected with the office than with its holder. It goes, therefore, with the duties and dignities and the loss of pontifical insignia could only happen if the papal dignity itself were lost. Nobody can withdraw the papacy from the pope, but he could renounce it freely himself, and his abdication would be valid without its being accepted by anyone (Canon 221); in fact the pope is accountable to no one and no one would be empowered to receive his resignation.

There is no doubt that the deposition of a validly elected pope is impossible. The sad circumstances which led to the "deposition" of certain popes, to the dismay of all Christendom, could only find their dogmatic and juridical solution in the free submission of the popes concerned.

As to the antipopes, it is evident that the usurpation of papal dignity and pontifical insignia come under one and the same judgment. Ciacconius, who otherwise took extreme liberties with regard to heraldry, is quite right in representing the arms of the antipopes without external ornament.

Apart from voluntary renunciation, there are only two reasons for the cessation of papal power. The Code does not mention them for they arise from the nature of the case. The first instance would be that of the certification of total insanity, which would be equivalent to death.*

The second, even more hypothetical case, would be the notorious personal heresy of a pope. The heretical pope would be *ipso facto* deprived of his jurisdiction; since he who is no longer a member of the Church can scarcely be its head.*

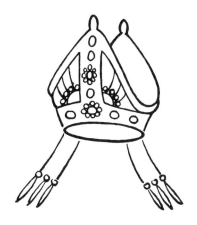

THE CARDINALS – In the old days, before they had received the red hat, Cardinals did not enter into their rights and so could not make use of their privileges. Nowadays, immediately following the publication of their nomination in the Consistory, they are in possession of their principal right – to take part in the election of the Supreme Pontiff. And since, according to Canon 233, § 1, they enjoy their privileges from that very moment they may also make use of the corresponding heraldic ornaments, even if for reasons of health, or any other reason, they are unable to be present at the ceremony of the giving of the red cap. (Plate 2; No. 2).

Cardinals may be deposed canonically, or may resign with the consent of the pope, who alone is competent to punish and depose them, (Canon 1557, § 1, 2° and 2227, § 1). In the course of history the deposition of a cardinal has not been rare; there has often been a formal declaration of the loss of the red hat and the insignia. If, for any reason, a cardinal renounces his dignity into the hands of the pope, he loses all the insignia, as in the case of deposition.

THE BISHOPS – Bishops are all those who have **received episcopal consecration**; that is, patriarchs, primates, archbishops and simple bishops, either residential or titular. Immediately after promotion, that is to say, as soon as their appointment has been officially published by the Holy See, they have the right to bear episcopal insignia in accordance with the liturgical law (Canon 349, § 1, 2°). How far does this extend? Cappello

* Wernz II, II, p. 353 & 354.

91

maintains that according to liturgical law the use of the crozier and proper pontifical ornaments is allowed only after consecration.* The Bishops' Ceremonial, however, allows them to wear the pontifical hat, adorned with green ribbon and tassels, before consecration.

Consequently, they have the right to ensign their shields with the green hat from the moment of promotion, but they cannot make use of mitre, crozier, or the cross, which, as has been seen, has become the heraldic sign of the episcopal order.

Canonical appointment to an episcopal see is preferably made during a secret Consistory, but since these do not often take place, and since bishoprics cannot long remain vacant, nominations are made as soon as necessary by papal Bull, and are published at the following Consistory. As soon as the Bull is received, and from the moment of preliminary official notification in the "Osservatore Romano", the prelate has a right to the episcopal hat. His arms may not be used for acts of administration, however, until after canonical possession of the see.

The resignation of a bishop from his diocese is only a renunciation of jurisdiction and not of his spiritual power, and so does not entail the loss of episcopal arms. A bishop who has retired from his bishopric has complete liberty to keep his insignia; he loses them only through specific arrangement with the pope, who may allow him, for instance, to set aside all external signs of dignity in order to devote himself to the monastic life. In the same way, only the Sovereign Pontiff himself may order the withdrawal of these insignia as the result of ecclesiastical punishment; it is reserved to him to judge bishops in *criminalibus* (Canon 1557, § 1, 3°). Even the most serious penalty cannot strip bishops and priests of the power conferred on them by consecration and ordination, it can only forbid the exercise of that power, and deprive them of the privileges of their status.

THE PRELATES – The prelates of the Papal Household, and all prelates of honour, receive their heraldic rights through the document of their nomination, or at the moment of taking the oath if they are required to go through this formality. That is the case, for example, with Protonotories Apostolic (D.15, No. 74).

---

* Cappello: Summa iuris canonici I. n. 387.

A prelate's privileges may be lost in different ways. First by authorised resignation. Then by loss of the office, if the prelacy is granted only *durante munere,* as for vicars-general (Canon 370, § 2), and prefects apostolic (Canon 308). Chaplains to his Holiness, on the other hand, lose all their rights on the death of the Pope. All prelates may lose their privileges through ecclesiastical punishment.

THE PRIESTS – Together with many authors (and as has been said already, against the erroneous opinions of certain others), we affirm that the right to an ecclesiastical black priest's hat belongs to every simple priest. They receive this right with the priesthood and cannot lose it except through ecclesiastical penalties bringing with them the loss of the privileges of the clerical state.

THE RELIGIOUS – The religious acquire the right to the heraldic symbols proper to them together with the clerical privileges which they enjoy already as novices (Can. 614). They lose these rights when they leave their order or congregation or when they are dismissed. Secularization and penalties which take away the clerical privileges would of course entail the loss of these rights as well.

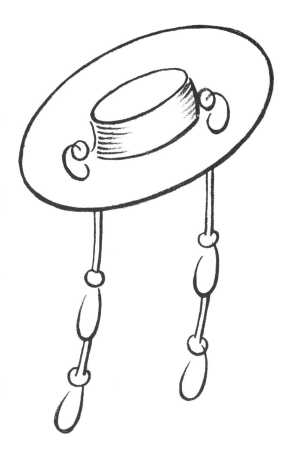

III

THE USURPATION OF ECCLESIASTICAL HERALDIC INSIGNIA

It is a part of the duty of ecclesiastical authorities to prevent the illegal use of clerical heraldic insignia. Usurping armorial signs comes under the same heading as the usurpation of ornaments and titles. Bartolus considers it a fraud (*crimen falsi*), and he is correct.

The usurpation of the pope's insignia was once considered a crime that deserved capital punishment, if it were committed with guile and the intent of misusing the

pope's jurisdiction. Today the law has become unnecessary. Nevertheless the Church cannot tolerate any abuse in this domain. The papal insignia have almost never been usurped in our times, but Saint Pius X still saw it his duty to condemn the wrong use of episcopal insignia by the lesser prelates.

Such abuse is deceptive, creating confusion and risking the loss of all value and usefulness of insignia.

A question which is frequently put is : "Can the usurpation of hierarchical insignia, in certain circumstances, become a right?"

It happens that some prelates use by custom insignia of a higher rank than that which they hold. The tiara of the patriarchs of Lisbon and the use of the patriarcal hat by some metropolitans come to mind, as does the use of the archiepiscopal hat by certain French and Swiss bishops. No apostolic privileges exist to justify these usages and their juridical status must be in doubt and worthy of examination.

How did usurpations begin? Presumably through ignorance of heraldic law or the belief that sufficient reason existed for the presumption.

Often the prelates were not themselves to blame. Not knowing their heraldic rights they relied on designers who offered their services. Many of these 'armorial manufactureres' were, and are, gravely ignorant of what pertains to the science of heraldry. They improvise according to their own uneducated ideas, or indiscriminately copy the wrong models. The prelates, for their part, reasonably suppose they could trust these self-styled specialists. Furthermore the mistake of, say, an ignorant engraver may be copied by successors of the prelate concerned, who would confidently adopt the heraldic customs of his predecessor, and defend as lawful the other's unconscious error. Given these conditions, is it possible to acquire the right to bear signs of dignity by prescription?

Cardial Patriarca
agradece ao seu distincto Autor a
oferta do exemplar de "Les Prodiges
d'Apocalypse de la Vierge de Fatima,
e felicita vivamente por ell: este li —
vrinho contem todo o essencial da historia de

Perhaps the absence of protests from Rome can be construed as tacit approval? In the first place, was Rome aware of the abuses? There is no doubt in the case of Lisbon and its tiara; Rome indisputably knew about it and did not rebuke the patriarch although the Archbishop of Benevento was forced to desist from a similar practice. Both were prominent; but if in some corner of the world a bishop makes use of an archbishop's insignia, can it be seriously claimed that Rome should know about it?

The most crucial question in this matter of prescriptive rights has yet to be asked. Are the insignia of ecclesiastical dignities subject to prescription at all? Canon 1509, 2°, excludes from prescription anything which can be obtained solely through apostolic privilege. All prelates' insignia, and even canons' insignia (Canon 409 § 1) are conferred only by the Holy See itself, and at times their heraldic use is explicitly forbidden because it is dependent on a special apostolic concession (D.11, No. 27 and D.15, No. 18).

There would be no solution, therefore, if Canon 63, § 2 did not very opportunely provide one. According to this Canon a century-old or immemorial possession of a privilege constitutes a presumption that the latter was actually granted. This juridical presumption dispenses the possessor from having to furnish proof, for what the law presupposes does not have to be proved (Canon 1747, 2°). Can the juridical basis of such privileges, in use for over a hundred years, be destroyed by a direct counter-proof? That must depend on the value attributed to the presumption established by Canon 63, § 2. If the opinion of highly regarded authors is to be admitted, then it is a question of a *praesumptio juris et de jure*, and not simply a *praesumptio juris tantum*. It must be concluded, there-fore, that even if the absence of a privilege is proved, the right of the present beneficiaries is in no way weakened.

A practice may not, then, be abolished if contrary to the general rule it has existed for more than a hundred years. There is no doubt about the tiara of Lisbon, the patriarchal hat of many an archbishop, and the archiepiscopal hat of Swiss bishops and others. These anomalies have become rights which could only be abolished by the formal prohibition of the Holy See, or if the concerned prelates spontaneously waived them, as the Swiss bishops now have done.

The arms of Mgr. Johannes Vonderach, Bishop of Chur, Switzerland. For a long time the Swiss bishops attributed to themselves four rows of tassels like archbishops. The reason given was that they did not belong to a province under an archbishop but were under the immediate jurisdiction of the Holy See.

95

The arms of Archbishop Hyginus Eugene Cardinale, Apostolic Nuncio to Belgium, Luxembourg and the European Economic Community, formerly Apostolic Delegate to Great Britain.

CHAPTER FIVE

I

THE HERALDIC LEGISLATION OF THE CHURCH AND ITS VALIDITY IN CONTEMPORARY CANON LAW

Heraldic legislation is much earlier than the present Code of Canon Law. The use of armorial bearings by clergy is so ancient that, centuries ago, it became necessary to bring it under some kind of general order. At the time of editing the Code almost everything was regulated by custom or law so it was not felt necessary to codify the heraldry of the Church and it was left untreated, save for seals. We may, therefore, question whether the Church's legislation is still in force in this matter.

Heraldic law derives entirely from common law, which remained in force in the Church as being in perfect agreement with the prescriptions of the Code.

There are also the numerous instructions of the Code with respect to seals which, as the legislators were clearly aware, are mostly armorial in character.

Further, prelates' arms featured in the official liturgical books, and this points the conclusion that the heraldic law of the Church is still in force, according to Canon 6, 6°.

Next, it is principally the rules and traditions of the Roman Curia which determine the use of arms, and according to Canon 328 these rules are valid though uncodified.

Moreover, two years before the promulgation of the Code, Benedict XV declared that bishops (D.16) are bound by the same heraldic prescriptions as those issued for cardinals (D.1) by Innocent X. This decree was not issued in order to be nullified immediately afterwards by the Code.

Finally, Pope Pius XI in the Apostolic Constitution *Ad Incrementum Decoris* of 1934, pronounced one of the principal documents of ecclesiastical heraldic law, the *Motu Proprio* of Saint Pius X, as still valid, (D.17, LV and LVI). The document was reprinted by the former Sacred Congregation of Ceremonial in 1942, and newly elected cardinals promise always to abide by all the decrees emanating from this same sacred congregation, in the new and abridged form of the oath they are obliged to swear. (D.18b.)

The only item of the heraldic legislation of the Church to be considered as abolished, by virtue of Canon 6, 5°, is the excommunication *latae sententiae* (automatic excommunication) issued by Innocent X against those who make, or cause to have made, cardinal's achievements adorned with crowns and temporal signs. This excommunication was lifted by the constitution *Apostolicae Sedis* of Pius IX in 1869, and Benedict XV also removed it from his decree concerning bishops of January 15th, 1915 (D.16.).

It is established fact that the heraldic usage of the Church, based on the law of office and insignia, is a symbolic representation of the whole ecclesiastical hierarchy, which remained the same before and after the Code. The Church's heraldic laws are above all modifications and clarifications of the common law, and their aim is to suppress any possible abuse. By means of these modifications, the ancient heraldic customs become part of modern law.

If a problem arises which is not covered by a statutory provision in heraldic law, then the customs and traditions must be consulted, especially those of the Roman Curia.

The rules promulgated by Apostolic Constitutions, the Decrees, *Motu Proprios* and Decisions of the Congregations, do not constitute a system of legislation based on a deep knowledge of heraldic principles; sometimes even the terminology is inadequate, and this is readily understandable for these decrees were issued over three centuries. They have been enacted in light of specific situations, and the thinking behind them has been dominated by the need to establish order at a particular moment.

Although it would be desirable to have clear and precise regulations governing the use of heraldic signs, these matters are of only secondary importance in the life of the Church. As far as uniformity and order is concerned the position is often no better in secular heraldry for it is difficult to differentiate the pure from the impure elements in the enormous output of heraldry. This demonstrates only too well the ignorance of many who commnly believe

The arms of Archbishop Guido del Mestri-Schönberg, Apostolic Nuncio to Germany.

The arms of Pope Pius XII

themselves qualified to devise arms and to write about heraldry. Bad heraldists create nothing but confusion as a result of their fragmentary knowledge, and their mistakes have regrettably influenced even the official heraldry of some countries.

The Church has been fortunate in keeping strictly to its own domain, concerning itself with the signs of dignity and refraining from making decisions on matters of blazon.

All the papal instructions regarding heraldry indicate the clear tendency to introduce order, to eliminate aberrations, to avoid usurpations and, above all, to maintain simplicity, a human quality well suited to clerics, and, at the same time, one of the fundamental qualities of good blazonry.

II

THE HERALDIC MARKS OF DIGNITY PROPER TO ALL RANKS OF THE HIERARCHY

1

1. The Arms of the Sovereign Pontiff

The following are the rules concerning the Pope's coat-of-arms :

The shield contains only the family arms of the Pope.

The shield is marked with the signs of papal dignity : the tiara and keys.

The tiara appears above the shield.

The keys, one Or the other Argent, are generally bound together by a cord Gules.

Gules and placed in saltire below the tiara, above or behind the shield.

It is not permissable to add any other external ornaments or decorations whatsoever to the papal arms. (*Plate 1; No. 1.*)

These rules have never been fixed by law, but are now faithfully observed on most of the heraldic monuments and in official representations of the papal arms. There are however exceptions to be found in older documents

98

for which engravers and lower functionaries might have been responsible.

Sculptural and architectural works rightly are allowed greater artistic freedom.

The insignia of papal dignity are unique; the ancient heraldic tradition of the popes, therefore, did not need the support of legislation. The Popes have acted so consistently in this regard as to render law quite superfluous, especially as only one person in the world is permitted to bear the insignia of supreme primacy. The classical elements of the official papal achievement have been maintained since more than five centuries, during which they have never been changed.

In their magnificent simplicity the Papal Arms are a model for all. Ecclesiastical heraldry has no place for ostentation and extravagance, or the needless and clumsy accumulation of external ornaments or other accessories.

The pleasing simplicity of the Papal Arms contrasts favourably with the arms of many temporal sovereigns, which sometimes sacrifice clarity and harmony in the clutter of external ornaments and a multiplicity of quarterings in the shield.

The Pope normally adds nothing to his family arms in his shield, the only exceptions among 92 armigerous Popes being Benedict XIII (1724-1730), Clement XIV (1769-1774), Pius VII (1800-1823), Gregory XVI (1831-1846), who were religious before their accession to the throne of Peter and marshalled their personal arms with those of the order to which they belonged. Additionally, Pope Pius X and John XXIII, both former Patriarchs of Venice, kept the lion of Saint Mark. (See *Plate 8; Nos. 32, 33, 34 and 35.* The development of the arms of Pope John XXIII.)

Ciacconi attributed arms to all the Popes as far back as St. Peter. The arms of Popes who lived before the age of heraldry are, naturally, purely imaginary. In Ciacconi's days it was a widespread custom to attribute arms to heroes and saints of a past age. Many famous men of antiquity have had arms invented for them, even Our Lord himself.

Some Popes of the pre-heraldic era have had attributed to them the later arms of their illustrious families, like the Counts of Tusculum, Dagsburg-Egisheim and Dollnstein-Hirschberg, the Dukes of Lorraine and the Counts of Burgundy. This attribution of arms has caused certain

Pope Pius XII with tiara and pallium.

Popes John XXIII and Paul VI wearing their coats of arms embroidered on both falls of the stole.

historical errors. Thus Catalani writes that Clement II (Suitger von Morsleben-Hornburg, d. 1047) was the first Pope to bear heraldic arms, a statement which is patently false.

The first authentic and still preserved heraldic monument of a Pope belongs to Boniface VIII (d. 1303). This monument is a marble slab with mosaic inlay in the Cathedral of Anagni. It twice shows his and his mother's shield, and between them the tiara and pavilion, depicted independently between the shields. The arms of John XXII (d. 1334) in Avignon Cathedral, are the first to show the shield marked with a tiara.

Also in Avignon there is carved, on a keystone in the papal palace, a shield of Benedict XII (1334-1342) ensigned by two small keys in saltire. His successor's (Clement VI, 1342-1352) arms are for the first time ornamented with the tiara and keys in saltire linked with a cord.

In the church at Beyssac, near Pompadour, some keystones have representations of the shield of Innocent VI (1352-1362) ornamented with a tiara between two sets of keys in saltire, and as is sometimes met with later, the keys are reproduced on the shield in chief.

On a fresco in the Palazzo del Capitano at Todi the arms of Innocent VII (1404-1406) are ornamented in the normal fashion with the tiara and keys in saltire.

At the begining of his Pontificate, Martin V (1417-1431) still had coins minted which bore his arms ornamented with the tiara alone. Later he definitively adopted the tiara and keys.

The renaissance baroque and rococo artists at times represented the papal arms with lions, children, angels or the Princes of the Apostles as supporters. As sculptural motifs the effect is not unpleasant. The official heraldry of the papal court has never accepted supporters although some strange exceptions do exist. However, and it can be rightly wondered whether it is in all respects proper to represent St. Peter as a squire to his successors!

The noble simplicity of the papal achievement has often suffered badly from those who altered the shape of the shield in order to make it more ornamental. Sculptors are especially guilty of the whimsical modification of its fine authentic form, so well suited to its use. They have brought to it all their ingenuity, and even virtuosity; yet often the overall impression is one of heaviness. Such artistic efforts were the unavoidable outcome of periods of great artistic creation, but, unfortunately many painters and engravers continue to imitate styles which are removed from that of genuine heraldry. The admirably consistent composition of the papal arms with their well-known three elements (shield, tiara and keys) is too often stifled in a veritable jumble of lines. These dated and decadent forms bear no relation to the original style of heraldry and are contrary to modern taste; they should never again be repeated. The pristine sources of heraldic art may be turned to for a style in keeping with the timeless function of heraldry.

It is evident that only the Pope has the right to ornament his arms with the tiara and keys. The papal insignia without the shield are used officially by the Congregations, Offices and Tribunals of the Roman Curia; by the Nunciatures and Apostolic Delegations, and finally by pontifical institutes. (*Plate 5; No. 20.*) Popes have often granted charges from their own shields to certain dignitaries of the Church as augmentations of honour, but never the tiara and keys together.

They also served in the formation of the Arms of the Church and the former Pontifical State. Official heraldry, however, has not carefully differentiated the arms of the Papacy from those of the Church, and the Papal States.

The papal banner is Or and Argent. To embroider the tiara and keys on either side of it is blatant offence against fundamental heraldic principles and taste. (*Plate 5; No. 22.*) To render them more visible and prominent they need contrast with the ground. The only way to obtain a well-shaped handsome papal Banner (impeccable historically and heraldically) is to put a shield gules charged with the papal insignia – tiara and keys – on the dividing line in the centre of the banner. (*Plate 5; No. 19.*) From the 16th Century on the coat of the Papacy may be blasoned: Gules a pair of keys crossed in saltire, one gold, one silver, tied gold, surmounted by a tiara silver, crowned gold.* To embroider the tiara and keys in gold and silver on the flag (or and argent) can only be qualified as heraldic daubery and should never have been done. (*Plate 5; No. 23.*)

Sometimes in the past the tiara appears over the shield. At other times the tiara or the pavilion appear in the shield

---

* Galbreath: Papal Heraldry, p. 25.

The arms of Bernard Jan Cardinal Alfrink, former Archbishop of Utrecht, Holland.

itself, above the keys. These combinations are seen on some papal standards, and relatives of the Pope have often received the pavilion and keys, as charges in their shields, augmenting the family arms. (*Plate 7; No. 28.*)

Pontifical publishers and suppliers to the Sacred Apostolic Palace, could use these arms by virtue of a special warrant, to show that they had the honour of working for the Holy See. Such concessions have ceased to be granted.

2

The Arms of Cardinals
(D.1., D.12., D.16., D.18.)

(*Plate 2; No. 2*)

The following rules have been established concerning cardinals' arms :

Cardinals ensign their shields with a red hat.

From both sides of the heraldic hat there hangs a red cord, fixed above by a tassel; the cord pierces the brim of the hat and ends in fifteen tassels arranged in five rows of increasing numbers :

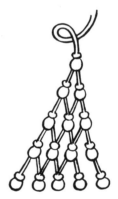

Cardinals are forbidden to add crowns, mantles, supporters, decorations or any other honorific signs to their achievements, with the exception of the crosses of the Order of Malta and the Holy Sepulchre.

Cardinals who are patriarchs, archbishops or bishops place a cross corresponding to their rank behind their shield, in pale, and they have the right to add a pallium, external to the shield, if they possess one as a reigning patriarch or metropolitan, although this is almost never done.

The red hat was conferred on cardinals, as a distinctive headpiece by Innocent IV in 1245, and in the Fourteenth Century it began to replace the mitre as an heraldic ornament, the latter having adorned their arms before that time.

When the aristocracy began to ensign their shields with crowns, the cardinals of noble origin followed their example, often preferring crowns to their red hats, or using both together. This custom, being an abuse contrary to the spirit of the Church, the Sacred Congregation of Ceremonies submitted the draft of a decree for the approval of the Pope on August 10th, 1644, in order to combat it. It was proposed that the Pope should oblige all concerned to be content with the title of cardinal and Most Reverend Eminence, in order to preserve fraternal equality among the cardinals.

In addition, to re-establish uniformity, the Pope was asked to order the cardinals to remove crowns and secular emblems from their shields, unless they were integral charges in their family arms, and, forbid under the pain of excommunication, sculptors, painters and engravers as well as their patrons, to represent the aforesaid temporal signs in the achievements of cardinals.

The cardinals who gave their names to this timely request certainly deserve all credit. They belonged themselves, for the most part, to the highest nobility. These were notably cardinals Capponi, Barberini, Spada, Corneli, Spinola, Branca, Montalto, de Medici, Colonna and d'Este.

Innocent X approved the decree at the Christmas Consistory of the same year. In order to prevent any loopholes, a clause was added declaring that the constitution *Militantis Ecclesiae*, through which the decree was promulgated, would keep its full force unless a succeeding pope should abolish it entirely.

The cardinals resident in Rome were obliged to accept the decree on oath within ten days, and four months was allowed to the cardinals not resident in Rome. The oath was preserved for a long time in its original form, and is still implicitly contained in the more recent abridged form. (D.18.)

The arms of Josef Cardinal Wendel, Archbishop of Munich, who died in 1960.

103

The arms of Paul Cardinal Bertoli.

The arms of Cardinal de Bonnechose, Archbishop of Rouen in 1858, are of a strange and heavily overloaded composition which is no longer permitted.

Up to the present the constitution *Militantis Ecclesiae* has never been revoked. On the contrary, Benedict XV re-enacted it by the already mentioned consistorial decree of January 15th, 1915, and extended it to patriarchs, archbishops and bishops unless a princely title was connected with their see. (D.16.)

In spite of the ex-communication which in days gone by threatened not only the artists but also those who ordered the work, the constitution was not observed without exceptions. Cardinal Henry Benedict of York, the last of the Stuarts (d. 1807), called himself Eminence and Royal Highness, and after the death of his brother, Charles Edward, in 1788, was recognized by the Jacobites under the name of Henry IX. He accepted the title of Majesty and had a royal crown placed over his cardinal's arms. Cardinal Gustave-Maximilian-Juste de Croy-Solre (d. 1844) did not hesitate to call himself prince and to ornament his shield (surrounded by decorations) with a princely crown, an archiepiscopal cross, and the cardinal's hat. French cardinals of the Second Empire generally used crowns, the senatorial mantle and civil decorations together with the usual ecclesiastical ornaments. The Sacred Congregation of Ceremonies did not stop at vain protests against such abuses. It ordered the removal without delay of all temporal signs from the arms of cardinals de Morlet, de Croy, de la Tour d'Auvergne and de Bonnechose de Boismorand on the façades of their titular churches in Rome.

Things have changed greatly since that time, and there is a general understanding of the Church's aim of achieving unity and simplicity in this matter. The cardinal's hat is itself a princely symbol, and temporal symbols have no further purpose alongside it.

However, the insignia of the Sovereign Order of Malta and the Holy Sepulchre are tolerated. These are orders of religious origin and their crosses are not considered temporal signs. The Order of Malta is, properly speaking, a religious order to which priests and laymen may belong as professed members and Knights of obedience.

The Order of the Holy Sepulchre is not a papal Order. Up to the second World War depended on the latin Patriarch of Jerusalem. For several years now it has had a cardinal as Grand Master. One of its principal aims is to support the works of the faith in the Holy Land. The

Holy See formally recognizes the religious character of this Order.

The number of tassels which adorn a cardinal's hat had long been considered as of no importance, and was not laid down. Since the pontificate of Pius VI (1775-1779), custom has fixed the number of tassels at fifteen per side. This number was made law by a decree of the Sacred Congregation of Ceremonies on February 9th, 1832. (D.13.)

Prior to this time the fashion was somewhat capricious, and, especially in monochrome, it was quite difficult to determine the exact hierarchical rank of the titular from the number of tassels. It is possible to find examples of hats having as many as twenty tassels on each side, and, with Crollalanza, it would be charitable to attribute these extravagances to the ignorance of the artists rather than the instructions of the prelates. The decree of 1832 is universally observed today.

Cardinals who are bishops, archbishops or patriarchs, place a cross in pale behind the shield according to their rank. It is an old and widespread custom, but no decree lays it down.

The other pontifical emblems, the crozier and mitre, were at one time more frequently depicted in heraldic art than is the case today. By right they belong to all cardinals (Canon 239, & 1, 13°), who could ornament their arms with them; but this was never the tradition of the Roman Curia, and in the interests of heraldic simplicity and clarity it is better not to add them to the arms of cardinals, as it has been ordered by Pope Paul VI in March 1969. (D.20.)

The arms of Mario Cardinal Nasalli Rocca di Corneliano.

3

The Arms of Patriarchs and Primates
(D.16.)

(Plate 2; No. 3)

At present the following are the regulations which concern patriarchs:

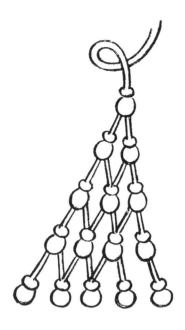

Patriarchs ornament their arms with a green hat from which hang two green cords ending in fifteen green tassels on each side.

Behind the shield they place a double-traversed cross in pale.

All signs of nobility or secular dignities and all decorations with the exception of the crosses of Malta and the Holy Sepulchre, are forbidden them.

Residential patriarchs possess the pallium and may use it as an external ornament.

The green hat placed above the shield is the pontifical hat already discussed. Palliot fixes the number of tassels on both sides of the patriarchal hat at ten, and most authors follow him in this. Certain well-known heraldists speak of a decree dating from November 3rd, 1826, which is said to fix the number of tassels at fifteen each side for the patriarchal hat, being the same number as for a cardinal's hat but green instead of red. Unfortunately, none of these authors indicates the source of their information. Every possible effort has been made to trace this alleged decree. It is not recorded in the lists of the Sacred Congregation of Ceremonies, and the Prefect of Ceremonies, the late Mgr. Carlo Respighi, stated that he, too, had looked for it in vain.

Did this decree ever exist? Ströhl and Fox-Davies affirm that, according to this decree, the cords and tassels must be intertwined with gold threads. This detail being without heraldic moment, one can take it that in reality it refers only to the ceremonial hat and not to its heraldic representation. In any case, nowadays the patriarchal hat is depicted with fifteen green tassels on each side.

The double-traversed cross and pallium are common to patriarchs and archbishops. The Roman Pontifical recognizes the heraldic use of this cross by these prelates, while St. Pius X forbids it for protonotaries apostolic. (D.15, No. 18.) There is no other legal disposition concerning the cross but its use, traditional in Rome, has been universal for centuries.

Patriarchs are forbidden to use emblems of secular dignity by decree of Benedict XV (D.16). Nevertheless, if they were titulars of a princely see, technically they until recently had the right to display its emblems.

In the past patriarchs, archbishops, bishops who were both assistants at the pontifical throne and Roman counts, sometimes put a count's coronet above their shields. But since this was an honorary ecclesiastical rank and not an hereditary or family title, the heraldic use of this crown was a matter of toleration rather than of right.

Benedict XV explicitly allows patriarchs to ornament their arms with the insignia of the Orders of Malta and the Holy Sepulchre. It should be repeated, however, that the predominant opinion among officials of the Sovereign Order of Malta is that only professed members have the right to place their shields on the cross of Malta, while the other dignitaries should content themselves with putting this cross below the shield – the concession for cardinals being an exception which the Sovereign Grand Master could grant *ad personam* to other Prelates as well.

On the heraldic use of the pallium there are no legal dispositions. Its use has been an increasingly frequent custom in certain countries. Residential patriarchs are free to use it, but it can scarcely be considered obligatory.

Can the principles relative to the achievements of patriarchs be applied to those of primates?

No ecclesiastical document deals with the armorial usage proper to primates. In general writers on heraldry make no mention of it. In any case there are no special external ornaments for primates. They must use either the insignia of archbishops or patriarchs. By title and honoured position, they seem to be more closely related to patriarchs than archbishops. Canon 271 places them in the rank of patriarchs, though below them in precedence (Canon 280); but heraldic difference is not founded on precedence. It, therefore, seems legitimate for primates to make use of the same heraldic external ornamnts as patriarchs.

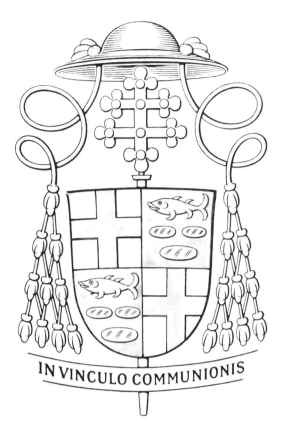

The arms of Mgr. Oskar Sayer, since 1978 Archbishop of Freiburg im Breisgau, Germany.

4

The Arms of Archbishops
(D.16.)

(*Plate 2; No. 4*)

The rules for patriarchs apply to archbishops as well, but we should note that there is a different number of tassels.

107

The arms of Archbishop Caesare Zacchi, former Nuncio to Cuba, now President of the Papal Academy for Diplomacy.

The arms of Archbishop Salvatore Papalardo, then Papal Nuncio to Indonesia, now Archbishop of Palermo and Cardinal.

Archbishops ensign their shields with a green hat pendent from which is a green cord on each side terminating in ten green tassels arranged in four rows :

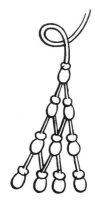

Behind the shield in pale, they place a double-traversed cross.

All secular indications of dignity and all decorations except the crosses of Malta and the Holy Sepulchre are forbidden them.

Residential archbishops possess the pallium, and could display it as an external ornament to their shield.

Palliot makes a distinction between the archbishop-primates and non-primates. The former he allows the external ornaments of the patriarchs, which were, according to him (in 1600), a green hat with ten pendent tassels on each side and the double-traversed cross. To archbishops who were not primates he gave a simple cross, and the same hat as for primates.

Not long afterwards Menestrier attributed to all archbishops the signs of dignity in common use today – the green hat with ten pendent tassels on each side and the double-traversed cross.

Formerly there were many archbishoprics and bishoprics with principalities and earldoms attached to them. Although, in our day, the nobiliary rights have almost disappeared, several archiepiscopal and episcopal sees on the Continent have preserved the titles, and Benedict XV left to their possessors the right to bear both ecclesiastic and the relevant nobiliary heraldic insignia. Later this right was abolished by Pius XII (D.19.), and Paul VI even forbade the heraldic use of mitres and croziers as additions to the hat and cross.

The prince-bishops' emblems were combined in various different ways. When bishops adorned their shields with the mitre and crozier exclusively, they simply put the temporal sword in saltire with the crozier as a sign of their temporal power.

In Germany there were in past times many prince-bishops whose achievements contained no ecclesiastical emblems whatsoever.

With the introduction of crowns and coronets for the different ranks of nobility, with a concomitant increase in heraldic splendour, prelates made increased use of crowns and mantles. Their shields, with mitre, crozier and cross, were often placed on a purple mantle lined with ermine issuant from a crown.

Often the hat was added too, thus combining hat, mitre and crown in one achievement. The cumulative effect may have been striking, but of doubtful taste. If a mantle and prince's crown were used, then the hat should have been excluded. The adorning of a shield with mitre, crozier and double-traversed cross, all upon a mantle, was quite enough to show the rank of a prince-archbishop.

It has to be noted that since the recent simplification of episcopal heraldry under the Popes Pius XII and Paul VI, most of these observations concerning secular emblems are of purely historical interest. (D.19 & 20.)

The arms of Dr. Franz König, Archbishop of Vienna; Cardinal since 1958.

The arms of Archbishop Silvio Oddi, former Nuncio to Belgium and Luxembourg; Cardinal since 1969.

The arms of Mgr. Hermann Schäufele, former Archbishop of Freiburg.

109

The arms of Mgr. Josef Schoiswohl, former Bishop of Seckau, Austria and now a Titular Archbishop.

The arms of Rt. Rev. Mario Joseph Conti, Bishop of Aberdeen.

The Arms of Bishops
(D.16.)

(Plate 2; No. 5)

The following are the regulations concerning bishops' arms:

Bishops place a green hat above their shields. The hat has a green cord each side, both terminating in six green tassels arranged in three rows:

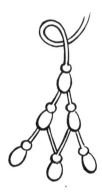

They place a simple cross in pale behind the shield.

All secular signs of dignity and all decorations with the exception of the crosses of Malta and the Holy Sepulchre are forbidden.

If a bishop has a pallium granted to him personally as a special favour, or by virtue of his see, he may use it as an external ornament to his shield.

Ever since the existence of a ruling concerning the number of tassels on a prelate's hat, six tassels have been commonly used for bishops. The official heraldry of the Church makes no distinction between bishops *immediate subjecti Sanctae Sedi* and others who belong to a metropolitan province; they all have the same insignia (Canon 349, § 1, 2°).

Since, on the one hand, the cross on its own signifies episcopal rank and, on the other hand, abbots are allowed the heraldic use of mitre and crozier, bishops have for some considerable time been increasingly abandoning the heraldic use of the latter. In Italy bishops rarely made heraldic use of the mitre and crozier, and

Roman custom dictated that the shield should be adorned solely with the hat and cross, as in the case of archbishops and patriarchs. Under Pope Paul VI that which was custom became a matter of special instruction (D.20.). It is preferable, of course, to have the minimum of ornaments and accessories in an achievement. The craze for adorning the shield in the most ostentatious way possible is always a sign of heraldic decadence. Archbishops and bishops can by the cross alone, without the hat, indicate unmistakably their hierarchical status. Beauty of symbolism, clarity of heraldic depiction, and a visual statement are thus perfectly conjoined.

6

The Arms of Abbots and Prelates Nullius

(Plate 3; No. 6)

It is not always possible to follow the order of ceremonial precedence in discussing ecclesiastical arms; that would have entailed dealing with the arms of certain prelates of the Roman Curia immediately after the cardinals, but a canonical and heraldic connection leads us to treat next the arms of certain prelates, whose duty from the point of view of jurisdiction is equal to that of the bishops – the abbots and prelates *nullius*. If they have not received episcopal consecration they belong with the lesser prelates. It should be explained that although episcopal power is conferred only through consecration it is nonetheless possible to grant episcopal jurisdiction independently.

Thus the Holy See grants to abbots and prelates *nullius* jurisdiction over the clergy and people of their territories. They are, therefore, equal to bishops in the matter of jurisdiction, but inferior to them in Holy Orders. Thus they are rightly called *semi-bishops* (*quasi-vel-semi-episcopi*).

At present no decree lays down anything concerning their arms. Their heraldic rights must be judged by analogy with those of bishops and the other lesser prelates. In jurisdiction abbots and prelates *nullius* are equal to

The arms of Rt. Rev. Cormac Murphy-O'Connor, Bishop of Arundel and Brighton, England.

The arms of Abbot Bernard Kaul of Hauterive. The arms are quartered: 1 – The Cistercian Order; 3 – the personal arms; 2 and 4 – the arms of the Abbey.

CONCORDES CARITATE

bishops (Canon 323 § 1): by ordination they are simple priests.

Since it is important in this matter not to diminish the rank of bishop, gained through consecration, the arms of abbots and prelates *nullius* must differ from those of bishops. Obviously, if a prelate has received episcopal consecration, as some of them have, then he may make use of the same insignia as all bishops. A doubt remains in the case of the others: since Canon 325 allows them the liturgical use of bishops' insignia, it may be wondered whether this privilege extends to heraldry. Mention of their arms in the literature of heraldry is unfortunately rare.

Ströhl, in his *Heraldischer Atlas*, describes the arms of archabbots and abbots *nullius* (who were not, by the way, equal in rank) as follows: — a green hat, six tassels pendent on each side, a crozier with veil and a mitre. In the twelfth volume of Herder's great lexicon there is an article on armory which says that the arms of the prelates *nullius* are represented in the following manner: a green hat with three green tassels pendent on each side, a veiled crozier and a mitre.

Rudolph Henggeler, O.S.B., in his article on heraldry in the fourth volume of the old *Lexikon für Theologie und Kirche* attributes the cross to all abbots, and, in addition, when they are abbots *nullius*, the green hat with six tassels on each side. According to him the arms of abbots and prelates *nullius* are, thus, equivalent to those of bishops.

Yet even though Ströhl gives no facts in support of his opinion, the author thinks him to be right. It is necessary, therefore, to try to adduce appropriate reasons.

According to Canon 325, abbots and prelates *nullius* wear episcopal insignia and the vestments and ornaments of bishops. This justifies their right to all episcopal heraldic insignia with the exception of the one symbol peculiar to the sacred character of a bishop. Thus they may ensign their arms with a green hat having six green tassels on each side, with the mitre and crozier, but the latter must be provided with a veil; many papal decrees have made this clear beyond all doubt. (D.2.)

The processional cross does not figure among the liturgical insignia proper to bishops. The *Ceremoniale Episcoporum* allows it only to patriarchs and archbishops. But, as we have seen, bishops have so made use of it in heraldry that the cross has become the symbol of episcopal order. The Code mentions it in Canon 274, 6°, on the subject of patriarchs, primates and metropolitans, clearly separating the right to have it carried before them from the right to exercise acts of jurisdiction, for these prelates may use this cross even in places where they have no jurisdiction. Consequently, the cross also figures in the achievements of simple titular bishops who have no administrative jurisdiction of their own. The only thing that prelates *nullius* have in common with bishops is jurisdiction; they cannot, therefore, place this cross behind their shields, a use that all bishops may rightfully employ because they are of the same *hierarchia ordinis* as patriarchs, primates and archbishops.

Because of certain abuses, Alexander VII established by decree twenty-one rules for the use of pontifical insignia by lesser prelates, none of which mentions the cross. Perhaps it could be objected that many things have changed since this decree of 1659, but Pius X, in the introduction to the *Motu Proprio* of 1906, still recognised the decree of Pope Alexander and wished to give it new vigour and new efficacy.

Finally, an argument of fact: cardinals who were not bishops had the right to pontifical insignia (Canon 239, § 1, 15°) and their right was certainly not less than that of the prelates *nullius*. In spite of that, they never adorned their shields with the cross. According to Roman usage, it belongs only to cardinals who are bishops or legates of the Pope.

Cardinals were forbidden to use temporal emblems in 1644, and in 1915 the ban was extended to patriarchs, archbishops and bishops, unless the emblems belonged to their see (D.16.), an exception which was later abolished by Pius XII (D.19.). Lesser prelates are not explicitly compelled to conform with these decrees. They certainly enter into the spirit of the Church, however, if they voluntarily observe them, for such conformity may be implicitly expected as their superiors, the higher clergy, are subject to these regulations.

We can, therefore, arrive at the following rules for abbots and prelates *nullius*:

a) They place a green bishop's hat over their shields, with a pendent green cord each side, both terminating in six tassels.

b) They might use a crozier instead of the cross.

c) If used, the crozier should have a veil.

The arms of the Abbot of Klosterneuburg.

EX LIBRIS

ST. HENRICUS

ST. PANTALUS

ARCHIVES DE L'ANCIEN
ÉVÊCHÉ DE BÂLE

*Ex Libris of the ancient Diocese of Basle.
(The Diocese was re-constituted 150 years
ago). Wood engraving by the famous Swiss
artist Paul Boesch (1889-1969).*

*The Arms of Abbots and Provosts with Mitre
and Crozier*

(Plate 3; No. 7)

Abbots and Provosts who have received the abbatial blessing have the following heraldic rights :

1. Their hats are black with black cords on each side
ending in six black tassels.
2. They had the right to the heraldic use of mitre and
crozier.
   According to the newest instructions they should
now, like bishops, omit the mitre. (D.20.)
3. Their croziers must have a veil.

Here we are dealing with the abbots who have the right
to use pontifical insignia, having received the abbatial
blessing (Canon 625). Among them are included all abbots
de regimine, i.e. the abbots primate, the abbots general
of monastic congregations, arch-abbots and the abbots
of exempt monasteries – all of whom are major superiors
(Canon 488, 8°). Retired abbots and titular abbots (who
exist in spite of Canon 515), have the same marks of
dignity.

This rule applies also to provosts, but solely to provosts
who have received the blessing, and excluding the minor
superiors, chapter dignitaries and parish priests who
sometimes bear the name provost without having the use
of pontifical insignia or the corresponding heraldic rights.

The hat with six pendent tassels (vert, purple or black)
on each side is universally considered in heraldry as the
sign of prelacy. It, therefore, pertains to all who are
actually prelates, i.e. all ecclesiastics of the secular and
regular clergy who possess ordinary jurisdiction in the
external forum (Canon 110) and to all honorary prelates
named by the Holy See (D.15, Nos. 18, 45, 68, and 79).

Prelates who are regulars do not, as a rule, wear purple.
Their ceremonial garb is normally black and, in consequence, their heraldic hats are also black. They bear the
same black hat as those provosts of the secular clergy who
have received the blessing, unless, in addition, they also
possess another honorary prelacy, or special privileges

which give them the right to wear purple. Some abbots wear an all-white habit, and are accustomed to ornament their arms with a white prelate's hat.

Abbots and provosts, following their blessing, have the right to the pontifical insignia handed to them in the course of the ceremony. They have been using them as heraldic ornaments since the Middle Ages. The old Roman Pontifical recognises this usage; as in the consecration of a bishop, the prelate receiving the blessing had to hand over a gift as a token of homage to the bishop giving the blessing. This gift consisted of two loaves and two small casks of gold and silver, adorned with the arms of the officiating bishop and with those of the newly blessed abbot and his monastery. There is confusion in the specification of the ornaments of these arms. The Pontifical only says that they are "arms with a hat, cross or mitre, according to the rank and dignity of each" (I, XV, § 6).

Until recently newly consecrated bishops offered to their consecrator two loaves of bread, two candles, and two barrels of wine, decorated with their respective coats-of-arms. The barrel on the right shows the arms of Dr. Franz von Streng; these are also depicted in a woodcut by Paul Boesch.

The arms of the late Mgr. Peter Schindler, a great scholar and writer from Denmark; he was a Prelate of Honour.

The crozier is not even mentioned despite the fact that it was the first symbol to come into heraldry from the liturgy, and nearly always as an external ornament. Unfortunately, it is rarely displayed as it ought to be. Several papal decrees, as already stated, require the lesser prelates' crozier to be provided with a veil. (D.2, D.3, D.14). Prelates are often loath to comply with this requirement. Scarcely a year had passed following Alexander VII's new regulations in this matter when the procurator of the Congregation of Monte Cassino tried to substantiate a claim, in Rome, that the use of the veil had never been customary in his congregation. Rome decided that the decree should be observed (D.3.) and other requests for a dispensation received the same answer.

The heraldic use of the veil was common in some countries and it offers the possibility of such fine effects for artists that some famous armorists have even used it for bishops.

As to the type of mitre, lesser prelates having it by privilege must conform strictly to the letter of the grant; if not explicitly mentioned the precious mitre must not be used (D.2). Although the most recent instruction (D.20) does not concern the abbots it would seem proper that they too should cease from using the mitre to ensign their arms if they make use of the hat. Not having the right to the episcopal cross it would be appropriate if they used a veiled crozier instead. If they prefer the mitre they should omit the hat. The intention of Pope Paul VI's prescript is to avoid pomposity, to make matters more simple and not to feature two headgears in one achievement.

8

The Arms of Major Religious Superiors

Abbots have the privilege of using pontifical insignia and it was therefore necessary to deal with their arms separately. We now turn to the rules for major superiors who do not have the right to pontifical insignia: the superiors general and provincials of most orders and religious congregations, their vicars and others on a par. (Canon 488, 8°).

The major superiors of exempt religious orders have ecclesiastical jurisdiction in both the internal and external forum (Canon 501). They are, therefore, prelates by right (Canon 110) and as such may use the heraldic symbol of dignity proper to prelates: the hat with six tassels pendent on both sides. Since they are "black prelates" their heraldic hats are black.

The black prelate's hat is thus the sign of the superior or ex-superior of an exempt religious order – if the constitution allows an ex-superior to keep his dignity as an *emeritus*.

This same hat is also worn by the Master of the Sacred Apostolic Palace, a prelate of the Roman Curia (traditionally a Dominican) who, being a religious, does not wear purple.

This hat belongs also to black prelates of the secular clergy, namely the titular protonotaries apostolic and those to whom common law allows the privilege, such as vicars general and capitular or those who possess these same privileges by way of a special concession, as the canons of certain chapters (D.15, Nos. 59-76).

The major superiors of non-exempt orders do not have jurisdiction in the external forum. They are not prelates, therefore, and may not use the hat except by virtue of a certain convention, which lacks any juridical foundation. Strictly speaking they should content themselves with the hat of an ordinary superior – black, with two black tassels pendent on each side.

The arms of H.R.H. The Prince George of Bavaria, Protonotary, Canon of St. Peter's, Rome; died 1943.

9

The Arms of Prelates "di fiocchetto"

(Plate 3; No. 8)

The prelates who were called *"di fiocchetto"* placed a violet hat over their shields, from each side of which was a red cord pendent, terminating in ten red tassels arranged in four rows.

The name of these prelates is derived from the tassel (in Italian: *Fiocco, fiocchetto*), formerly decorating the heads of their horses in the grand cavalcades on special

EX LIBRIS
B. F. H.

The ex libris of Mgr. Bernard F. Hack, Protonotary Apostolic, Canon of Santa Maria Maggiore, Rome.

occasions or in ceremonial processions. In the earliest period of knightly heraldry, the horse was decorated heraldically as well as its rider : it is, therefore, not surprising that the horses bore a decoration on their gala harness symbolic of the prelate's position of honour. There were only four of these high ranking prelates of the Papal Curia : the Vice-Camerlengo of the Holy Roman Church, the Auditor General and the Treasurer General of the Apostolic Chamber and the Majordomo to His Holiness.

These last three titles are no more granted. Only the office of the Vice-Chamberlain has remained and is at present held by an archbishop.

No written law exists on the subject of the arms of these prelates. They were determined by the traditions of the Papal Court and enjoy the protection of law (Canon 328). Monsignor Barbier de Montault, and Count Pasini Frassoni, having lived under these traditions, are guarantors of their authenticity (Barbier, b, 88; Pasini, c, 15).

The traditions of the former Papal Court are a confusing and intricate matter for the layman, and in his *Motu Proprio* "Inter multiplices" (D.15) St. Pius X exemplified and simplified the legal rules which govern the heraldic signs of dignity for most prelates. Yet there is one point which has remained obscure owing to the fact that the terminology is not technically heraldic. The author of the *Motu Proprio* forgot to indicate the exact colour of the prelate's heraldic hat. He indicates only the colour of the cords and tassels (D.15, No. 18); it would be easy to suppose the hat to be black, like the prelate's hat described immediately before (No. 17); but this supposition contradicts the tradition according to which the prelate's heraldic hat is violet.

Further on, (No. 68) the author of the *Motu Proprio* deliberately chooses his words and states that the colour of the heraldic hat of titular Protonotaries Apostolic must differ from that of other protonotaries. Although the actual hat the titular protonotaries wear is all black, he says of the heraldic hat : "over their shields they may place a hat, but it must be black with pendent cords terminating in six tassels each side, also entirely black."

This "but" makes the author think that the hat of the other protonotaries is not of the same colour; it seems to indicate a distinction. By tradition, in fact, it should be violet. Otherwise, for the first time, we would have an

118

apparent contrast between the hat actually worn and the hat displayed heraldically.

The author has made painstaking investigations in order to clarify this point. Heraldry, of course, does not slavishly follow the natural or real colour of objects, but it would be odd if this unusual heraldic colour should have been chosen for the prelate's hat unless a violet hat had been worn. Presumably this was notably the case during grand ceremonies, and, above all, in the cavalcades typifying an age long past. This hypothesis did have a basis in fact, and the author finally found proof of it: Moroni (IX, 183) describes the arrival of the cardinals at a Consistory and tells how they surrounded the one about to receive the red hat. "The latter (the newly-elected cardinal) rode on a mule with the hood of his cloak over his head. On the hood he placed the hat he had worn before being made a cardinal; that is, an entirely green hat if he was a bishop, or violet if he had been a prelate. . . ."

This eye-witness account confirms that the violet hat of heraldry once existed and was worn in public.

The arms of a Protonotary Apostolic of Innsbruck, Austria.

10

The Arms of Protonotaries Apostolic

(Plate 3; No. 9)

With the *Motu Proprio* "Pontificalis Domus" (28th March 1968) the system of prelatical honours was simplified. There are now Protonotaries Apostolic, Prelates of honour and Chaplains to His Holiness, all other honorary titles having been abolished.

St. Pius X declared that all Protonotaries, except titular ones, "may place a hat over their shields with cords having twelve tassels which hang six on one side and six on the other, of red colour, without a cross or mitre."

According to the evidence already rendered this would mean:

1. They place over their shields a violet hat, having six red tassels pending on each side.

2. The use of the episcopal cross, mitre and crozier as external ornaments is expressly forbidden them.

The arms of Mgr. Alfred Newman Gilbey, Prelate of Honour, Chaplain of Honour to the Sovereign Military Order of Malta. The Maltese Cross appears in an unconventional manner.

The honorary or titular Protonotaries Apostolic ensign their shields with a black hat having six black tassels on each side (D.10 & D.15, No. 68), for they are prelates *extra Urbem* (D.15, No. 63). This title may be granted individually or to an entire chapter (D.15, No. 59 & 61).

To repeat VICARS GENERAL und VICARS CAPITULAR have the same privileges for the duration of their office (D.15, No. 62; Canon 370 § 2 & Canon 439).

In recent years many bishops with the approval of the Holy See have appointed VICARS EPISCOPAL with special duties in the diocese. We find it logical that they should use like vicars general the black hat with six black tassels on either side, unless they have a higher prelatical title granted them personally by the Pope.

11

The Arms of Prelates of Honour
(D.15.)

(Plate 4; No. 10)

The Prelates of Honour, formerly Domestic Prelates, place a violet hat over their shields with violet cords terminating in six violet tassels each side (D.15, No. 79).

The language of the *Motu Proprio* is, as already said, lacking in technical precision. It decrees that violet is the only colour allowed, but only mentions the tassels and cords. As we know already, however, the prelates of the Roman Curia have a violet heraldic hat and reference to the *Motu Proprio* settles that the number of tassels is six on each side. (No. 18). Thus, the hat, cords and tassels are all violet in colour.

12

The Arms of Chaplains to His Holiness

(Plate 4; No. 11)

The Papal Chaplains, who, like prelates, bear the title Monsignor, are appointed to the personal service of the Sovereign Pontiff, ranking below prelates of honour. Their office ceases on the death of the Pope who appointed them. Prior to the recent simplification of such titles there were both Privy Chamberlains and Chaplains to His Holiness.

Privy Chamberlains were divided into four classes and the Chaplains to His Holiness formed five classes. These rank within ranks, which in any case brought about no heraldic differencing, have been swept away.

There are no legal regulations concerning the arms of Chaplains to His Holiness and no colour was designated for the hat they used to wear in Rome. Outside Rome they were permitted to decorate their hats with violet cords terminating in violet tassels. Count Pasini attributed to them, therefore, as heraldic ornament, a black hat with violet cords and six violet tassels each side. This seems to accord with ecclesiastical heraldic usage and propriety, but Monsignor Battandier sees six tassels for a Chaplain as an abuse and reduces them to three on each side. Ströhl, Henggeler and all those who follow them are of the same opinion. It is an open question, but certainly the hats of Chaplains should be distinguished from those of prelates, and this is conveniently achieved by making the formers' black with the cords and tassels being violet.

The arms of H.R.H. Prince Maximilian, Duke of Saxony, Prelate of Honour.

13

The Arms of Canons
(DD. 5, 6, 7, 8, 9, 11, 12, 15, 17)

(Plate 4; No. 12)

Canons have always involved the Holy See in a great deal of work; even more than the protonotaries whose

The arms of Father Augustinus Heinrich Count Henckel von Donnersmarck, a Regular Canon (Ord. Praem.); he is a Knight of Honour and Devotion of the Order of Malta; the Maltese Cross appears in this achievement.

affairs had to be taken in hand at least three times a century on average, though these could, at least, be treated as a unit. Things are more complex when it comes to the canons. The Church has had to come to terms with the appetite of ecclesiastical chapters all over the world for privileges of varying sorts. Fortunately the innumerable particular insignia and vestments granted to cathedral and collegiate chapters of all countries, *ad incrementum decoris et solemnitatis cultus divini*, do not find expression in as many heraldic differences. The relatively few differences that exist can be explained the more easily and clearly when the bases for them are known.

More often than not it is a case of whole chapters being granted membership of one of the classes of prelates already mentioned, with all the concommitant privileges.

Even to this day there is an heraldic distinction between canons of major basilicas and those of minor basilicas; and between canons belonging to privileged chapters and ordinary canons; these latter, to increase confusion, are divided into cathedral, collegiate, secular, and regular canons.

There have been differences of opinion among authors concerning the heraldic signs of dignity for canons; but in spite of all these apparent difficulties it is possible to regulate the heraldry of canons notwithstanding the embarrassing multiplicity of types, precedents and opinions.

The first essential distinction is that between ordinary and privileged chapters. It may be concluded with some certainty that the heraldic external ornament for ordinary canons is the black hat with three pendent black tassels each side. Any usage that differs from the above must be firmly grounded in the lawful possession of special privileges.

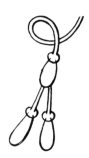

Only the Holy See can grant special privileges. Bishops have no right to grant their chapters new insignia, or change in any way at all the insignia and ornaments approved by Rome. It is also inadmissible to extend the privileges of one chapter to any others in an arbitrary fashion, as these privileges are always granted for special reasons, attached to a place, a specific sanctuary or chapter.

In addition it should be remembered that these privileges must be interpreted in the strictest possible sense (D.11, No. 5; D.15, No. 80; & Canon 67). Nothing apart from the black hat with three tassels each side may be used, even as an heraldic ornament, unless the privileges grant the heraldic use of other insignia in an explicit manner (D.11 and D.12, No. 27).

For example, some chapters had the privileges of Supernumerary Protonotaries Apostolic granted them (D.15, No. 13 and D. 17, LIV), others possessed the privileges of Protonotaries Apostolic *ad instar* (D.5; D.15, No. 42; D.17, LVI). All the canons of these chapters, provided that the required individual conditions were fulfilled for each of them (D.15, Nos. 14 and 34), had the right to ornament their arms with a violet hat having six red tassels pendent on each side in exactly the same way as Protonotaries Apostolic.

The canons whose chapters possessed the privileges of domestic prelates (D.15, No. 80) or of Privy Chamberlains, had a similar right to adorn their shields with the corresponding hat.

Yet another peculiarity should be noted : by apostolic privilege the dignitaries, or even all the canons, of certain chapters were granted the favour of wearing a mitre (DD. 6, 7, 8, 9, 11, 12), yet they could not use it to ensign their shields unless they were granted the specific privilege of doing so (D.9; D.11, No. 27; and D.12, XXVII). When those so privileged used the mitre heraldically they had to give up the hat (D.6 and D.8).

Finally, some chapters possessed the titles of count or baron for each member, as was the case with St. John and St. Justus at Lyons, St. Julian at Brioude, St. Peter at Mâcon, the Cathedral of Milan, and St. Barbara at Mantua. These chapters could display, as of right, their arms complete with a count's or baron's coronet, after the fashion of those bishops who occupied a see with a nobiliary title. All such practices now belong to the past.

The arms of Canon Lèon Dupont-Lachenal, Regular Augustine Canon of Saint-Maurice.

The arms of Father Raoul Miorcec de Kerdanet, O.P., former Prior of the Dominican Convent of the Holy Sacrament in Paris. His arms are quartered with those of the Dominican Order, and the cross fleurette of the Order also appears.

Honorary canons of a chapter have the same insignia and honorific prerogatives as the chapter canons (Canon 407, § 2).

Regular canons come under the same heraldic principles as the seculars, since both bear the title and possess the appropriate insignia and vestments.

14

The Arms of Deans and Minor Superiors

(Plate 4; No. 13)

Count Pasini is wrong to quote the decree *Cum innumeri* (D.10) as applicable to deans, for it concerns titular Protonotaries, a dignity which has no connection with the office of dean but concerns vicars general and vicars capitular.

The following are the traditional heraldic rules for deans, non-exempt major superiors, and all other minor and local superiors who are not prelates by right: by custom they have a black hat with two black tassels pendent each side. These two tassels may hang from a median knot, side by side, or they may hang one above the other.

Neither law nor custom has anything to say about such diocesan officials as chancellors, secretaries, and archivists. If they have not personally received an ecclesiastical title with proper heraldic rights they should use only a simple priest's hat.

15

The Arms of Priests

(Plate 4; No. 14)

Some authors allot parish priests, chaplains and other priests having a benefice or a permanent post, a black hat with one black tassel pendent each side. Priests who have no permanent post are, by these authors, denied the right to ornament their arms with an ecclesiastical symbol. It is more fitting, and correct, to consider the black hat with one tassel each side as the sign of the priestly dignity, and it is certainly better that a priest who wishes to ensign his shield should use an ecclesiastical hat rather than a helmet or coronet. Those who object to a simple priest using an ecclesiastical hat hold this opinion arbitrarily, and without the support of any ecclesiastical decision, code or regulation. It must be remembered that all priests belong to the same ecclesiastical order and are thus possessed of equal sacerdotal and other privileges.

The arms of a Polish priest, Dr. Edward Grzymala, who died in Dachau.

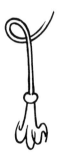

16

The Arms of Abbesses and Lay Religious

Abbesses and mothers superior are not members of the clergy, and have no jurisdiction in the Church. Neverthe-

The arms of the Reverend Mother Jeanne-Marie Comte, former Abbess of the Cistercian Convent Notre-Dame de la Maigrauge in Fribourg, Switzerland.

The arms of the late Fra (Count) Ferdinand von Thun und Hohenstein, Knight of Justice in the Order of Malta, a professed Religious.

The arms of Dame Bridget More, a descendant of Saint Thomas More, elected Prioress of the English Benedictines (in exile) in 1653.

less, they possess authority in religion, and exercise a maternal power over their subordinates.

The Roman Pontifical presupposes that abbesses are in possession of a seal, and consequently of a coat-of-arms. They share with monks and lay brothers the right to surround their shields with a rosary. Abbesses in the old religious orders who have received the blessing, carry a crozier during certain official functions in their convents, for example in processions, and for centuries have made heraldic use of it, alone or with a rosary.

It need hardly be added that an abbess's crozier must be veiled. As far as the artist is concerned, the veil could not be more apposite. It helps him fill the empty space between the crozier's crook and the shield with elegance.

No one denies other religious, lay brothers or sisters who are armigerous, the use of the rosary to ornament their shields, this being an apposite sign of the religious.

In England and France Abbesses (and Abbots) ignored, or did not know about the rule of the veil so often to be insisted upon by Rome. The English Abbesses used the unveiled crozier and a crown above their shield.

Prioresses and above all the Abbesses of the Brigittine Order (Ordo Sanctissimi Salvatoris, founded by Saint Bridget of Sweden), represented in England by Syon Abbey at South Brent, Devon (founded in 1415 at Isleworth in Middlesex) mark their shield, like the Brigittines all over the Continent, with a crown only. There is no crozier, but the shield is often flanked by two palm branches. (*Plate 7; No. 31.*)

As this is a centuries old custom there is no reason to change it as far as heraldry is concerned.

Abbesses and Prioresses sometimes surrounded their shield with interlaced cords like other ladies, thus indicating that it was a lady's coat-of-arms. This was particularly helpful if the charges could not easily be placed in a lozenge, as for instance in the case of Prioress Bridget More of the English Benedictines in Paris, a descendant of Saint Thomas More.

17

The Arms of Corporate Ecclesiastical Bodies

Since the Church started using heraldry, many corporate bodies, collegiate or non-collegiate, have adopted it as well; this custom is still kept up today. There are records of arms of orders, religious congregations, chapters, confraternities, monasteries, dioceses, ecclesiastical territories and offices.

If they are good heraldry their shields in no way differ from other achievements; but many of the recent "heraldic" creations are regrettably tasteless pious caricatures.

Many bishoprics and abbeys have ancient and beautiful arms, which often evoke their foundation with eloquence, as well as recalling their former properties, ancient feudal dominions or past legal jurisdiction. The same applies to Orders and Congregations with historic arms. If the latter have been in use for over a hundred years they enjoy legal protection on the grounds of immemorial right and custom, while the new ones need the approval of the competent ecclesiastical authority. Johannes Kirchberger reviewed the achievements of religious orders in 1895, but his collection is incomplete and lacking in critical judgement. Some of these arms are still contested, as Hauptmann, Waltz and Féret have shown in the case of the Dominican Order – which, up to the present, makes use of two different achievements. The ancient shield of this order is very fine and simple, even when placed upon a cross flory-gyronny, as it sometimes is; however, all too often the lower part is covered with a motley collection of charges, which ruin the achievement's heraldic value.

The countless achievements of the institutes and offices of the Church cannot be considered within the limited scope of this study. Suffice it to say that the Church's heraldic regulations in general do not deal with these arms and their external adornments, but one relative regulation exists from the ancient Congregation of Bishops and Regulars, dated November 20th, 1611, which says that chapters do not have the right to arbitrary use of the mitre and crozier in their achievements.

The arms of the Diocese of Gurk in Austria.

A rubber stamp of the arms of the Diocese of Oslo.

The seal of the Hospital of St. Marien-wörth dedicated to the Blessed Virgin Mary. The shield shows symbols of the Blessed Virgin Mary.

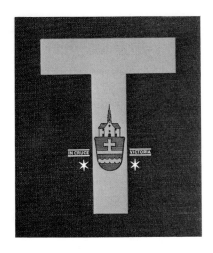

In general, bishoprics, abbeys, provostries, and chapters ornamented their shields quite simply with the emblems of their prelate. This procedure, although acceptable, created inconvenience through the resultant ambiguity: for a person who is unacquainted with the charges displayed on the shield it is impossible to detect whether the arms belong to the prelate, the office or the community. This difficulty is now diminished as Cardinals, Patriarchs, Archbishops and Bishops no longer use the mitre and crosier in their achievements, but only the hat and cross, while Abbots consequently should use their hat and crozier.

The dioceses and abbeys and their offices may now without danger of confusion mark their shield respectively with mitre, cross and crozier or mitre and crozier. There is no prescription or prohibition existing in this regard. On the other hand, these offices need their seals and stamps every day.

Prelates often marshal their personal arms with those of their diocese or abbey either by quartering or impalement or, if one of the coats-of-arms is already quartered, by putting a small shield in pretence. Whether one should prefer quartering or impalement cannot be decided upon uniformly in advance. If an artist possesses real heraldic sense he will in each case choose the marshalling which gives the finer result otherwise he might draw out or compress the given charges too much and his product will be ugly and unharmonious.

The custom of displaying the arms of the diocese has fallen into disuse in some countries. This is to be regretted for practical and aesthetical reasons.

(Top)

The arms of the Franciscan Brothers of the Holy Cross, represented in Germany, Netherlands, U.S.A. and Brazil. Above the shield appears a representation of their foundation chapel.

(Above)

The seal of La Roche College, Allison Park, Pennsylvania, U.S.A.

(Right)

Azure seme-de-lis and two crosiers in saltire or. The flag of the Praemonstratensiens, also called Norbertines or White Canons: Candidus et Canonicus Ordo Praemonstratensis, founded in 1120.

CHAPTER SIX

HERALDRY IN THE ORIENTAL CHURCHES IN UNION WITH THE HOLY SEE

In the oriental churches, that is to say, the churches of Eastern Europe and the Near and Middle East where they follow a rite other than the Latin Rite, heraldry is a rather recent introduction. The reason for this is that in most countries where the oriental rite is predominant heraldry is not autochthonous, save for those that were formerly part of ancient Russia or the Austro-Hungarian Empire.

However, it has become increasingly common for the oriental uniate bishops to follow the practice of western prelates and assume arms on their elevation to the episcopacy.

It is obvious that, in drawing up their arms, oriental prelates should follow the same due process as all the others, according to the principles which will be indicated later. This does not prevent them from adopting emblems customarily favoured in their own countries. On the contrary, they should be encouraged to choose those charges which will give a properly oriental flavour to their achievements, provided that they are appropriate to heraldic representation, as are most animals, plants, trees, flowers, leaves, fruits and other commonplace objects. Landscapes, crucifixes, statues, chalices surmounted by radiant hosts, texts, letters, machines, and other vulgar or prosaic objects, should at all costs be avoided, even though appalling examples can be found in ecclesiastical heraldry.

Obviously, oriental prelates make use of liturgical symbols when ornamenting their arms. It is, therefore, a question of establishing whether the pontifical insignia of these prelates are the same as those of the Latin Rite, or whether they have their own special form. In fact, the Eastern mitre and crozier are often different in form from those commonly used in the West, and these differences find expression in the heraldic display, thereby giving an evocative character to the achievements of oriental prelates.

Six principal rites can be distinguished in the Uniate

The arms of His Beatitude Hemaiagh Petrus XVII Ghedighian, Armenian Patriarch of Cilicia.

The arms of the Maronite Patriarch Anthony Peter Khoraiche; he uses the arms of the See only. The shield is simplified for the sake of clarity. Heraldic charges should never overlap.

A

The arms of Mgr. Cyril Mogabgab (1855-1947), since 1899 Greek-Melchite (Byzantine) Bishop of Zahleh and Forzul, in 1925 elected Patriarch of Antioch.

B

The arms of Mgr. Demetrios Metropolitan of Alep (Beroea).
DT – MB = DemeTrios Metropolites Beroias.

C

The arms of Mgr. Florian Grebnitzky, Archbishop of Polotsk, (died 1762).

D

The arms of Bishop Ceslaus Sipovich, since 1960 Visitor Apostolic of Belorussians in Great Britain and Western Europe. His shield is identical to that of the Princess Sapieha. It is quite frequent in Slavonic countries that families who are administrators of, or in a patron-bondsman relationship to a feudal lord, use his coat of arms.

Churches. These are the Armenian, Byzantine, Chaldean, Coptic, Maronite and Syrian Rites.

As is the case in the Latin Church, different ranks in the hierarchy have different liturgical vestments, but since only the higher prelates have adopted heraldic usage we need only mention the "sensu proprio" pontifical insignia, leaving aside all other varieties of liturgical vestment.

In the Uniate Churches of the Byzantine Rite (Greek, Russian, Melkite, Ruthenian, Yugoslav, Bulgarian, and Rumanian) the bishop's headgear for Pontifical Mass differs from that of the Latin Rite mitre, being rather like a royal or princely crown made not of precious metal but a stiff material adorned with gold, brocade, and precious stones, or embroidered with flowers, crosses and other images or icons.

The form of the pastoral staff is also quite different. It does not curve over at the top in a crook, but terminates in two serpents facing each other between which there is usually but not always a cross.

The Armenian bishops wear a mitre which is almost identical to that of the Latin bishops, and their crozier is also the same. Cardinal Agagianian, Patriarch of Cicilia, used four staves: the episcopal crozier, the patriarchal staff terminating in a globe surmounted by a cross, the patriarchal double-traversed cross and the doctoral staff, which has serpents like the Byzantine crozier. His successors use the same insignia.

Armenian priests and deacons wear a headpiece which resembles the Byzantine bishops' mitre. It is a round tiara issuing from a crown flory and surmounted by a small cross. It is rare, however, to find Armenian clerics using coats-of-arms.

Syrian Catholic bishops adopted the mitre and crozier of their Latin confreres, as did the uniate Chaldeans and Maronites.

Save in the case of the Armenian patriarch just mentioned one can discern two main tendencies in the heraldry of the oriental prelates. The first is followed by the churches of the Byzantine Rite, and the second is followed by the other oriental churches whose prelates have adopted the Latin form of mitre and crozier.

In consequence, the latters' arms are ornamented in just the same way as the Latin prelates': ideally it would be preferable for them to make use of the mitre and

A

ΔΜ ΤΒ

πρᾶος καί ἰsχυρος

B

C

D

ZA CHRYSTA I CARKVU

The arms of Mgr. Joseph Horbacki, Belorussian Orthodox Bishop of Vitebsk. (Designed after a very mediocre wood engraving of 1652).

crozier in place of (not together with) the pontifical hat, which is not worn in the East.

With prelates of the Byzantine Rite three different customs can be distinguished :

1.   Some of them decorate their arms in the same way as the Latin prelates.

2.   Others make use of external ornaments of mixed origin. An example are the arms of Archbishop Florian Grebnitzky of Polotsk (d. 1762) whose simple shield (without indication of tincture) was charged with a cross accompanied by two crescents. This prelate ornamented his arms with a pontifical hat in the fashion of the period, and with an archiepiscopal cross in the manner of a Latin archbishop : but he added a Byzantine crozier and mitre, together with a coronet indicating family nobility. This usage was not at that time forbidden for the bishops.

Of mixed origin is also the achievement of the Maronite Patriarch. He uses the mitre crozier and pallium like many Latin prelates in the past. In addition he uses a treble patriarchal cross otherwise not used in church heraldry.

We show (*Plate 6; No. 24*) the achievement of Andrew Roman Alexander Count Szeptyckyj (d. 1944) who in 1900 was elected Ukrainian (ruthenian) Metropolitan of Lemberg and was the direct predecessor of Cardinal Slipyj.

If the Roman hat were omitted this achievement could be considered as properly oriental. Count Szeptyckyj's predecessor Metropolitan Sylvester Sembratovicz put (also improperly) the Roman hat above the oriental achievement. In addition he used an ermine lined mantling like a continental prince-bishop which is entirely wrong. The oriental mantling is not a princely attribute but a liturgical garment, a kind of a cloak or cope called "mandyas".

3.   The third custom is the most correct and most properly oriental. As an example we give here the coat-of-arms of a Melchite (Byzantine) Bishop, Monsignor Cyril Mogabgab (d. 1947), who in 1925 at the age of seventy, was elected Patriarch of Antiochia. It is not easy to find coats-of-arms of oriental prelates with heraldically correct charges. Bishop Mogabgab's is quite good. His shield is marked with the cross

and the greek crozier. The whole is placed on the *mandyas* issuant from a Byzantine pontifical crown or mitre.

The liturgical colours are not established among the orientals as they are with us. The mitre (crown) is sometimes gold or silver brocade or pinkish-violet and gold embroidered.

The *mandyas* is of the same colours and lined mostly with bright yellow silk. To make it look as a liturgical cope rather than a robe of estate or a prince's mantle it might be better not to have it hitched up on the sides.

It must be admitted that this achievement has a character entirely of its own and makes a splendid impression. It may be considered as a model achievement for all oriental prelates of Byzantine Rite.

Evidently it is equally correct to keep the crozier and cross under the *mandyas* as most oriental Prelates do, and as it appears in the arms of the Melchite Metropolitan, Demetrios of Alep (consecrated in 1903). He bore : Gules an oak tree or, displaced to the sinister : on a chief azure three bees of the second.

These charges constitute a good example of arms perfectly yet unemphatically suited to the motto PRAOS KAI ISXYROS (in Latin suaviter et fortiter), the bees being symbols of gentle sweetness, and the oak depicting strength.

The uniate Copts could also use their mitre, the cope and their cross and crozier. Their present Patriarch Cardinal Stephanus I Sidarouss however uses a letter-heading with his shield ensigned with the crown-mitre only. Evidently, being a Cardinal, he could also, as an alternative, have the cardinal's hat and the cross, like other Cardinals.

———————

In the ORTHODOX CHURCHES the use of coats of arms is much less frequent. As an example we give here the achievement of Joseph Horbacki, Orthodox Belorussian Bishop of Vitebsk in 1652. The marks of dignity are the byzantine Mitre and serpent crozier and the bishops staff or rod used in the orthodox Churches.

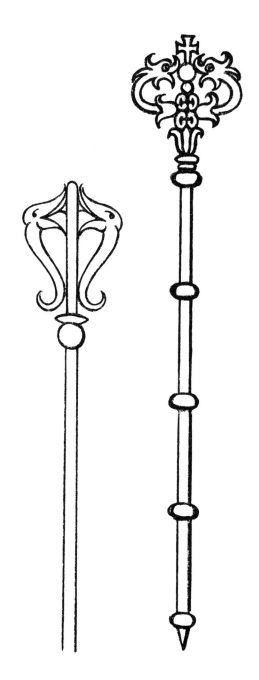

(On opposite page)

The arms of Cardinal Stephanos I Sidarouss, Coptic Catholic Patriarch of Alexandria. He ensigns his shield with the Oriental mitre only, not using his Cardinal's hat. The shield is rather overloaded.

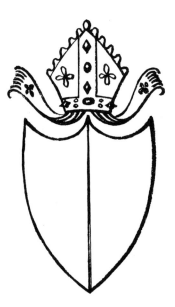

CHAPTER SEVEN

HERALDRY IN THE CHURCH OF ENGLAND

Archbishops and Bishops of the Church of England usually ensign their shields with the precious mitre (and not the hat) (*Plate 6; No. 26*) generally over the unadorned arms of their See. It is permissible for them to impale their personal arms with the arms of the See, as in Archbishop Fisher's arms depicted in the 1978 edition of Boutell's Heraldry (Plate XXII, 2). Two croziers in saltire can be placed behind such shields. Warren represents the arms of the See of Canterbury with the mitre over the shield and the double cross and crozier in saltire behind it.

The arms of His Grace The Rt. Hon. and Most Rev. Archbishop of Canterbury.

For the non-episcopal anglican Clergy there were, until very recently, no official rules governing the ensigning of their shields. With an Earl Marshal's warrant this deficiency was remedied by the introduction of what the Heraldry Gazette lightly, but not slightingly, called a "new line in hats". It is worth reprinting the editorial comment of the official News-Letter of the Heraldry Society (No. 69, May 1977) on the Warrant and its application :—

"For some decades certain clergy of the Anglican Communion have used ecclesiastical hats in place of helms and crests in much the same way as is done in the Roman Church. The trouble has been that this practice, having the blessing of neither the Church nor the heraldic establishment, has been very much a D.I.Y. exercise.

In Scotland precedents for certain hats have been created and followed. Thus a clergyman has a black hat with a single black tassel on either side, unless he is a Chaplain to the Queen, when the tassels and the cords they hang from are red. The Dean of the Chapel-Royal has three red tassels on either side of his hat. Bishops have green hats with six and Archbishops with ten tassels pendent on either side.

In England only one hat appears to have been painted on a grant to an Anglican clergyman, when a green Roman Archbishop's hat appeared on the patent granting arms to the Rt. Reverend Spence Burton, Bishop of Nassau. An Archbishop's hat ensigned the arms granted to the Most Reverend William Godfrey, Archbishop of Westminster but thereafter the English Kings of Arms felt that as they had no official knowledge of what hats should be used, it would tidy things up if some research could be done and a whole range of appropriate headgear laid down by an Earl Marshal's Warrant, This was done in 1967 and details can be found in post-1967 editions of Boutell's Heraldry.

Recently certain Anglican clergymen suggested that a range of Anglican hats should also be established by Earl Marshal's Warrant. The Archbishop of Canterbury with the support and approval of other prelates, agreed that the use of hats in place of helms and crests was unexceptionable and asked the Earl Marshal if he would issue a Warrant. This he did on 21st December 1976.

His Warrant prescribed "appropriate Ecclesiastic Hats which may henceforth ensign the Arms of the Clergy of the Anglican Communion in lieu of Helms and Crests". The operative word in the Warrants is 'may' for the use of hats is permitted but not made mandatory, because for every high churchman who craves a fashionable hat there must certainly be a hunting parson who would not be seen dead in one.

The arms of Rt. Hon. and Rt. Rev. Lord Bishop of London.

PLATE V

19. The Pontifical (*Papal*) *Insignia* are the tiara and the two keys.
20. The arms of the *Papacy* and *Vatican City* show the papal insignia on a shield gules.
21. The *Pavilion* is ready in all basilicas for the eventual visit of the Pope and has become the emblem of the basilicas. The pavilion with the keys but without the tiara is used during any vacancy in the Holy See (*sede vacante*) by the Cardinal Camerlengo; (see Chapter Three, IV, 3).
22. The *Papal Flag* is gold and silver, gold being next to the staff on the heraldic right (dexter). The emblems of the Papacy being also gold and silver, the obvious and correct thing to do from the heraldic and aesthetic point of view, and for the sake of clarity, (so absolutely essential in heraldry), is to put the arms of the Papacy, the red shield with the tiara and keys, in the middle of the flag.
23. The papal insignia of gold and silver are too often embroidered on the silver (or white) part of the flag. Whoever did this first must have been totally lacking in heraldic and aesthetic feeling. On a coloured ground, the gold and silver papal insignia stand out as they should; on a white background the silver is lost.

PLATE VI

24. The arms of a *Ukranian Archbishop*: Andreas Roman Alexander Count Szeptyckyj (1865-1944), Ukranian Metropolitan of Lemberg from 1900, and immediate predecessor of Cardinal Slipyj as Archbishop-Major of Lemberg. This achievement is not purely oriental, for the archiepiscopal hat is a Latin element. It is nevertheless attractive.
25. The arms of the *Prince Grand Master* of the Sovereign Military Order of Malta, His Eminent Highness, Fra Angelo de Mojana di Cologna. The arms of the Order are quartered with the family arms of the Prince Grand Master. He is a professed Knight with religious vows, hence the rosary around his shield. The princely mantle issuing from a sovereign's crown is black and often 'semé-de-lis' argent.
26. The arms of an *Anglican Bishop*, the Bishop of Salisbury. Anglican Bishops use the precious mitre as their mark of dignity.
27. The arms of the *Dean* of Westminster Abbey, The Very Reverend Dr. Edward Frederick Carpenter, Dean since 1974. The Dean of Westminster Abbey is also Dean of the Most Honourable Order of the Bath, hence the pendant badge. His shield is ensigned by a Dean's hat. The arms of the Abbey are impaled with the Dean's family arms.

19

20

21

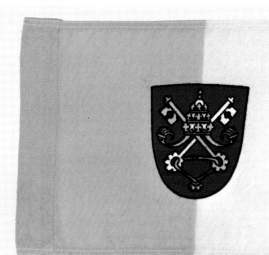

22

23

24

25

26

27

28

29

30

31

32

33

34

35

PLATE VII

28. The flag of the *Papal Swiss Guard* : a cross argent, in the four quarters
   1) the arms of the reigning Pope Paul VI; 4) the arms of Pope Julius
   II (1503-1513), Giuliano della Rovere, founder of the Swiss Guard, 2
   & 3) the colours of the Guard; gules, or and azure; in the centre of
   the cross the arms of Commanding Officer, Colonel Dr. Franz Pfyffer
   von Altishofen.

29. The arms of a *Dame of the Equestrian Order of the Holy Sepulchre*,
   Mrs. Dorothy Hanley, Pittsburgh, Pennsylvania. Her husband, Mr. Ed
   Hanley is a Commander of the Order of the Holy Sepulchre and a
   Knight of the Sovereign Military Order of Malta. A lady's shield can
   be oval or lozenged. With these charges the oval seems more
   appropriate.

30. The shield of the *High Master of the Teutonic Order*. The *Ordo
   Teutonicus*, (*Fratres Ordinis Teutonici Santae Mariae in Jerusalem*),
   was founded in 1190. The Order had a great, albeit bellicose, history.
   Until 1918 its High Master was an Austrian Archduke. Since 1854 the
   Order also had the help of sisters in nursing the sick. After 1918, for
   the first time, a priest was elected High Master. In 1929 the Order
   was given a new religious rule and spiritual discipline was re-
   established. Today its aim is parish work and special care for the sick,
   the unhappy and the poor. The High Master, who has the rank of an
   abbot with mitre and crozier, resides in Vienna (Austria).

31. The arms of *Syon Abbey* and the *Bridgettine Order*, (*Ordo Sanctissimi
   Salvatoris*), founded by St. Bridget of Sweden (about 1346) and
   confirmed by Pope Urban V in 1370. Syon House was founded in
   1415 by King Henry V at Twickenham, Middlesex. After more than
   300 years of exile (since 1594 in Lisbon) the sisters, now settled at
   South Brent in Devon, returned to England in 1861. The long exile
   explains why the achievement is not typically English. The Bridgettine
   Abbesses did not use the crozier and instead of the rosary, proper to
   Religious, we have here palm branches flanking the shield. Only the
   charges reveal that the arms are unquestionably ecclesiastical. The
   charges are : the five bleeding wounds of the Saviour, the crown of
   thorns and a cross with a host in the centre. The lion is believed to
   come from the family arms of St. Bridget. The Order had about 80
   Monasteries and Convents all over Europe. Today only 11
   Bridgettine Convents survive. A modern branch was founded in 1911
   by the Swedish convert Elizabeth Hesselblad with houses in Rome,
   England, the United States of America, India, Sweden and
   Switzerland. They use a crowned shield with the same charges as
   Syon Abbey.

137

PLATE VIII
THE DEVELOPMENT OF THE PAPAL ARMS OF POPE JOHN XXIII

32. Pope John XXIII was elected in the late afternoon of October 28, 1958. A few days before the election, the author of this book started painting Cardinal Roncalli's shield with the papal tiara and keys. It took him less than two hours that evening to complete the work and despatch it by airmail. Twenty hours after Pope John's election, the painting was in his hands.

    The shield depicted only the personal or family arms of the Pope without the lion of St. Mark which, as Patriarch of Venice, he had in chief. Pope John was well aware of the fact that only five previous Popes had alien charges in their shields: four of them belonged to religious orders which was a valid reason for combining their family arms with those of their respective orders.

    In the case of Pope Pius X it was probably the ignorance of those who designed the coat-of-arms for him that caused them to use the shield he had in Venice and simply replace the patriarchal cross and cardinal's hat with the papal tiara and keys. Venice is one of the very few places in Italy where diocesan arms are used.

33. However, for reasons of his own, and as I had expected, Pope John wanted to keep the lion of St. Mark and made this known to me. I therefore made a further design with the lion in profile and sent it to Rome before leaving to attend the Pope's coronation. When receiving me in audience on the eve of the great day, Pope John said: "This lion with those teeth and claws has too fierce an aspect. He is too *transalpine*! Could you not make him look more human?"

34. As a result, during the night of November 3, I designed a third version with the lion in half profile, the mouth shut and the claws withdrawn. When I presented it to the Pope he said: "Now we are getting nearer to what I have in mind but let the lion be seen full face and not looking so lean; he needs to have a little more body!"

35. Thus the final version with an almost smiling lion was produced and received full approval from Pope John, who ordered its immediate publication.

The prescribed hats, all of which are different from any prescribed for Roman Clergy and all of which are black."

The Earl Marshal's Warrant is addressed to the Corporation of the Kings, Heralds and Pursuivants of Arms of the College of Arms. Its wording is :

The arms of The Duke of Norfolk, Premier Duke of England and Hereditary Earl Marshal.

"Whereas the Most Reverend Father in God Right Honourable Frederick Donald, Lord Archbishop of Canterbury, hath represented unto me that certain Clergy of the Anglican Communion are desirous of ensigning their Armorial Bearings with Ecclesiastical Hats in lieu of Helms and Crests and that in his view it would be proper and acceptable for those Clergy who desire so to ensign their Armorial Bearings to be permitted so to do and hath further represented unto me that certain types of Ecclesiastical Hat have been prescribed by those learned in ecclesiastical tradition and in the law customs and usages of Arms and that such usage has the full approval of the said Most Reverend and Right Honourable Archbishop.

Now therefore I, Miles Francis, Duke of Norfolk, Companion of the Most Honourable Order of the Bath, Commander of the Most Excellent Order of the British Empire, upon whom has been conferred the Decoration of the Military Cross, Earl Marshal and Hereditary Marshal of England do hereby authorize and direct you to record these Presents and the annexed schedule prescribing the appropriate Ecclesiastic Hats which may henceforth ensign the Arms of the Clergy of the Anglican Communion in lieu of Helms and Crests and for so doing this shall be your Warrant.

Given under my hand and Seal this 21st day of Dec. 1976.

NORFOLK E.M.

Then follows the Schedule of Ecclesiastical Hats which may be used in lieu of Helms and Crests by certain Clergy of the Anglican Communion :—

"Deans   may use a black hat having three red tassels pendent from purple cords on either side

"Archdeacons   may use a black hat having three purple tassels pendent from purple cords on either side

"Canons, Honorary may use a black hat having three
Canons, Canons red tassels pendent from black
Emeritus and cords on either side
Prebendaries

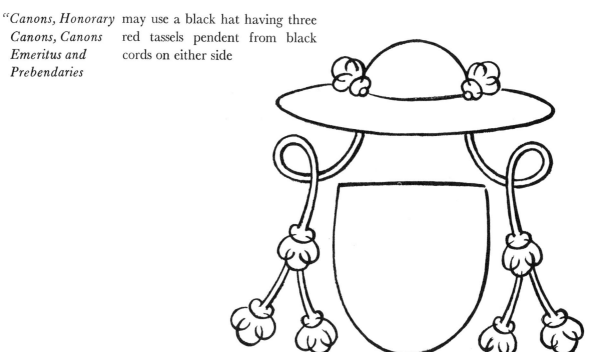

"Priests may use a black hat having one
black tassel pendent from a black
and white cord on either side

*"Doctors of
Divinity*   may use the hat appropriate to
their degree the cord being interlaced with a skein of red

*"Members of
Her Majesty's
Ecclesiastical
Household*   may use the hat appropriate to
their degree charged on the front
of the crown with a Tudor Rose
proper

"Deacons   may use a black hat without cords
or tassels".

Included in our illustrations is a series of sketches of Anglican hats that all differ in shape yet accord strictly with the terms of the Earl Marshal's Warrant. They constitute an affectionate attempt to show how variety of form may be achieved in heraldry by skilled and correct artistic freedom in order to prevent slavish following of the first good examples. We have too often experienced how badly the unimaginative imitation of set patterns has abased catholic church heraldry.

The seal of Richard Copley-Christie, M.A., Chancellor of the Diocese of Manchester from 1872-1893. As Chancellor he impaled his arms with that of the Diocese.

The arms of the Rt. Rev. Lord Bishop of Southwark.

IUSTITIA ET CARITAS

B.B.H. 1956.

144

CHAPTER EIGHT

I

ADVICE ON DRAWING UP NEW ARMS FOR PRELATES

We have learnt from history and Canon Law how the Church allows all its priests access to the highest offices, regardless of origins. Many reach the most exalted of dignities without being armigerous and since they require seals, and therefore arms, they are obliged to create, or cause to be created, new achievements.

As made evident *inter alia*, the Church allows them complete liberty in the matter of the shield itself, and newly elected prelates have no other regulations to observe save those of the art of blazoning. At the same time they have to take account of the heraldic law ensuring exclusiveness, which prevents the adoption of the arms of another without permission, and, of course, in countries where there is a heraldic office (College of Arms) they should have their shields approved by it.

Unfortunately, such is the ignorance and so great are the blunders too often involved when new arms are devised, that it seems appropriate to give a few guidelines on this subject.

First of all – repeating the advice already given – it is necessary to seek help from an expert, rather than trust one's luck to the numerous engravers and *soi-disant* heralds who offer their services whenever a new prelate is elected. Though many of them may be good craftsmen, they are seldom learned about heraldry. By relying on such purveyors one can inadvertently become an object of ridicule and be saddled irrevocably with defective arms which offend against good taste and do no honour to their bearer's aesthetic judgment.

Many ecclesiastics regrettably hanker after designs which are directly opposed to heraldic good sense. They have their shields decked out with pious images, often inspired by some motto taken from Holy Scripture, or alluding to their christian names. In this way they try to obtain canting arms, but such attempts mostly reveal nothing but the crudest naivity. In 1951 only 23 out of

The arms of Mgr. Theodor Hendrik Zwartkruis, Bishop of Haarlem; quartered: 1) the arms of Haarlem Diocese; 2 & 3) the canting arms of Bishop Zwartkruis (= black cross); 4) alluding to a legendary eucharistic miracle in Amsterdam.

(On opposite page)

The arms of Mgr. Josef Streidt, a most excellent bishop; he died in 1961 as a result of broken health due to his years in a concentration camp. In his arms he wanted to represent the fight between good and evil.

IN LABORE REQVIES

A SOLIS ORTU

UT OMNES UNUM SINT

51 Cardinals had arms a heraldic scholar could approve of. Some had them devised by a *carabiniere* who was not too bad a painter!

Count de Saint-Saud regarded it to be a sign of grave disrespect to charge one's arms with images of the Saviour, the Holy Virgin or the Saints.* It is well to remember that arms can be reproduced on the commonest of objects: on carpets, mosaics and floor-tiles on which people will walk; or embroidered on cushions that will be sat upon. Also, it is in practice almost impossible to do justice to the features of saints, given the small dimensions of the shield when made into a seal, or printed as a letter heading on writing paper.

Another error common among ecclesiastics is to have arms which are too cluttered. The oldest, purest and most beautiful arms are always the simplest. The overcrowding of a shield makes it seem the more artificial; in the place of a clear and distinct blazon, one has instead a mediocre rebus representing the life-history of the holder.

Saint-Saud quotes the description of one bishop's achievement as: *Azure, the child Jesus proper, vested purple, nimbussed Or, charged with a heart inflamed of the same, pointing to it with his left hand, blessing with his right, seated on a cloud Argent, resting on a chalice Or, supported by a cloud Argent.* These arms are an attempted allusion to the legendary eucharistic miracle of Douai (in 1254). Anyone can see that they are un-heraldic, and their blazoning is forced to attempt a des-cription of charges conspicuous more for acrobatics than other qualities.

A third mistake of some frequency in recent eccles-iastical heraldry consists of placing initials or whole in-scriptions on the shield. This practice is completely opposed to the true heraldic diction and expression and reminds one of a commercial advertisement or trade mark.

Having pointed out the pitfalls it is possible to ennumer-ate those basic precepts which, if followed, will lead to good new achievements.

Firstly, one should devise arms that are simple and original, and the charges should fill the field of the shield in a manner that is both harmonious and well-propor-tioned, not necessarily symmetrical.

---

* Armorial des Prélats français 1908, p. 10.

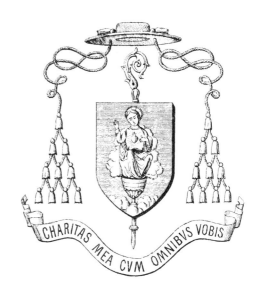

(*Left*)

A

The arms of John Francis Cardinal Dearden, Archbishop of Detroit, are cant-ing; they should not be impaled with the arms of his diocese because the charges would be deformed thereby; they could, however, be quartered.

B

The arms of Sergio Cardinal Guerri are impaled. The charges are very suitable for impaling.

C

The arms of the late Peter Tatsuo Cardinal Doi, Archbishop of Tokyo, who chose charges of a specific Japanese appearance.

D

The arms of Archbishop Bernard Yago of Abidjian are a good example of employing typically African devices.

ROSA MYSTICA

TURRIS EBURNEA

DOMUS AUREA

REGINA
APOSTOLORUM

STELLA MARIS

If a prelate's achievement is to be combined with an already existing achievement of a diocese or abbey, the choice of tinctures for the new achievement must not clash; if possible one should avoid juxtaposing colours which are too much alike. It is precisely the use of contrast which makes the shield stand out and sets off the charges displayed on it.

The person who wishes to recall a patron saint in his arms should first establish the characteristic attribute of this saint. There is, for example, a rich assortment of crosses to choose from – like those of St. Peter, St. Andrew, St. James, St. John, St. George, St. Anthony, St. Maurice etc. – each of them indicative of a particular saint. There are universally recognized symbols for many of the saints: the angel, lion, ox, and eagle represent the four Evangelists; the keys evoke St. Peter; the sword, St. Paul and other martyr-saints; the knife, St. Bartholomew; the shell, St. James; arrows, St. Sebastian; deer antlers, St. Hubert and St. Eustachius; the lamb, St. Agnes; the dragon, St. Michael and St. George; the dog, St. Dominic; the crow, St. Benedict; the lion, St. Jerome; the sceptre or crown, a canonized king or queen; the tiara, a canonized pope; the crozier or mitre, a canonized bishop or abbot; the heart, St. Augustine; the lily, St. Joseph; and so on. All these signs lend themselves well to heraldic representation and preclude tendencies to extravagance, provided one does not attempt to represent them proper but keeps to a style which is in conformity with the authentic art of heraldry.

As already mentioned, depicting the image of the Holy Virgin in one's arms should be avoided in new creations; but if it is wished thus to recall the Mother of God there are plenty of different titles for Her which are highly suited to heraldic representation. Consider the invocations of the litany: mystical rose, tower of David, tower of ivory, house of gold, ark of the covenant, gate of heaven, morning star, star of the sea, and many others. These may be used with propriety and dignity.

There exist, however, many old examples of arms with the figures of Christ, the Holy Virgin and Saints represented in ecclesiastical shields and, as the arms of Salisbury diocese show (*Plate 6; No. 26*), they can look fine and dignified.

II

THE ARTISTIC REPRESENTATION OF ECCLESIASTICAL ACHIEVEMENTS

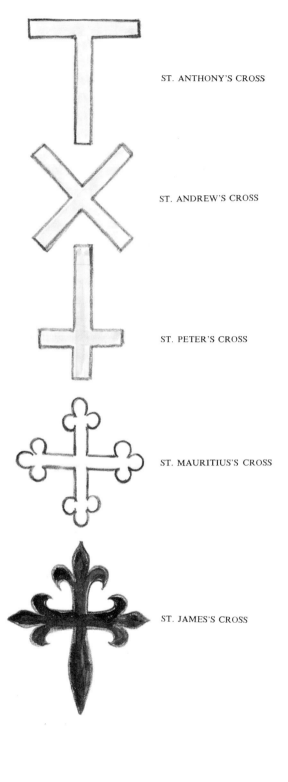

ST. ANTHONY'S CROSS

ST. ANDREW'S CROSS

ST. PETER'S CROSS

ST. MAURITIUS'S CROSS

ST. JAMES'S CROSS

The legal control of the use of insignia of rank is indispensable, but it would be absurd to try and fix the grouping of charges and method of representing ecclesiastical arms by absolute stereotypes. The Church, in fact, has never done so, and customs and traditions do not require it. However, there are some who believe that certain modes of expression are to be preferred in church heraldry, and always followed as constituting, in a sense, some sort of obligatory curial style.

It is precisely this slavish imitation of frequently defective models which has long been the gravest fault of ecclesiastical heraldry. This dependence has its roots in the uncertainty of the "bucket-shop heraldist" who is usually lacking in a sound knowledge of the science of blazoning. But such a lack of knowledge can hardly be supplemented by imitating models drawn up in equal ignorance. It is also a fact that it is exceedingly difficult to copy an achievement well if one is not an expert, for the unpractised eye can easily overlook certain essential details. Instead of studying heraldry properly such people continue to grope in the darkness of their fragmentary knowledge and preconceived ideas. Even when exercising their hand at new creations, they remain but copyists, for the freedom of the real artist – and never was this so true as here – burgeons only in the soil of a perfect knowledge of the subject.

It is, of course, important that the rightful owner's signs of dignity should be represented with exactness and clarity, but the artist has perfect freedom concerning the arrangement of the external ornaments, the shape of the shield, the style of the hat and tassels, or the interlacing of the cords, and many other ways.

Yet the depictions most frequently seen are not always beautiful; indeed, the contrary is so much the case that they have incurred the criticism of outstanding authors, who reach the point of writing, for instance, of the "prelate's ugly hat". The ugliness of the hat derives only from poor artistic skill. The author does not believe that one

149

The arms of the famous author Louis de Wohl and his wife Ruth; he was a Grand Officer and she is a Dame Commander of the Order of the Holy Sepulchre.

(Extreme left)

The arms of Edward J. Kelley, a Knight of Magistral Grace of the Order of Malta; (Pittsburgh, Pennsylvania, U.S.A.).

(Left)

The arms of D. C. R. Pehrson, Knight of Magistral Grace of the Order of Malta; Knight Officer of the Savoyard Order of SS Maurice and Lazarus.

(Right)

The arms of an old Swiss family, Hophan; the shield with appropriate marks of ecclesiastical dignity was used by Dr. Beda Hophan, former Abbot of Disentis, and also Dr. h. c. Otto Hophan, a Capuchin Friar and well known religious author.

is condemned to observe such bad design as an object of immutable tradition, or the copying of it as an exercise in ecclesiastical obedience. Only one thing is indispensable : the external ornaments of the shield should indicate the rank of the rightful bearer, without the possibility of a mistake. They may, and should, be represented as beautifully as the innate gifts of the artist permit.

The cross, crozier and mitre were generally placed below the hat, but no competent authority has forbidden a more original arrangement. One knows of superb achievements in which the cross rises above the hat, thus corresponding much better with natural proportions, for the cross is taller than a man. In his richly illustrated account of the Council of Constance, von Richental often placed the ornaments gracefully beside the shield and it is open to all true heraldic artists to exercise their skill and freedom of judgement similarly. It is preferable to use traditional, or orthodoxly symmetrical, compositions for official purposes, but in pursuit of the highest attainable ideals in decorative ecclesiastical heraldry the scope is essentially limitless. The sole end of the Church's heraldic legislation, to reiterate the basic point, is to ensure simplicity and the clear distinction of hierarchical rank, while preventing any illegal use or usurpation of insignia. This places no embargo on beauty; rather should all who are privileged to serve the Church through the science and art of heraldry ever strive to add to its dignity by their efforts.

The arms of the town of Puerto de la Cruz, Tenerife. These arms, like many civic shields, have an evident religious meaning. This is very frequent, not only in Catholic countries; in Finland, for example, one fifth of the arms of towns and villages show crosses, symbols of the Holy Virgin or of other saints.

The crusading arms of the Barons von Hessberg are most suitable for impaling. These arms can still be seen scratched in a rock of Mount Sinai.

151

VAN DUREN

EX LIBRO AMICORUM ET ILLUSTRORUM HOSPITUM QUEM BRUNO
BERNARDUS HEIMO ARCHIEPISCOPUS TIT. XANTHIENSIS SANCTIS-
SIMIQUE PONTIF. MAX. DELEGATUS DILECTIS SUIS SIBIQUE IN
MONUMENTUM ARMORUM IN SIGNIIS ORNAVIT.

APPENDIX

DOCUMENTS
BIBLIOGRAPHY
INDEX

DOCUMENTS
(D.)

D.1. *Innocentius* X., 19 Dec. 1644, Constitutio Apostolica "Militantis Ecclesiae regimini", BR, XV, 338 ss.

Constitutio super titulo et insignibus S. R. E. Cardinalium.

Militantis Ecclesiae regimini, meritis licet imparibus, per abundantiam divinae gratiae praepositi, inter gravissimas multiplicesque apostolicae servitutis curas, quibus assidue premimur, in eam peculiari studio incumbimus, ut inter S. R. E. Cardinales, quos tamquam reipublicae christianae cardines, et clarissima catholicae Ecclesiae lumina, omnium virtutum splendore ceteris praelucere decet, fraterna servatur œqualitas, unde sincerae caritatis affectu sese invicem prosequantur, et, dimissa omnium saecularium rerum cura, nonnisi pro communi eiusdem Ecclesiae bono ac omnipotentis Dei gloria vigeat inter eos laudabilis aemulatio.

Hodie siquidem in Consistorio Nostro secreto dilectus Filius Noster Aloysius tit. S. Laurentii in Lucina Presbyter Cardinalis Capponius nuncupatus, decretum per Venerabiles Fratres Nostros eiusdem S. R. E. Cardinales Congregationis Caeremonialis praepositos emanatum, Nobis retulit tenoris subsequentis, videlicet; S. Congr. Caer. . . . in qua interfuerunt Rev. mi Domini Aloysius tit. S. Laurentii in Lucina Presbyter Card. C..pponius, Franciscus S. Laurentii in Damaso Presbyter Card. Barberinus, Bernardinus . . . Card. Spada, Fridericus . . . Card. Cornelius, Jo. Dominicus . . . Card. Spinula, Franc. Maria . . . Card. Brancatius, Franciscus . . . Card Montaltus, Carolus . . . Card. Medices, Hieronymus . . . Card. Columna, Raynaldus . . . Card. Estensis, censuit enixe Sanctissimo Domino Nostro supplicandum ut, . . . districte praecipiat S. R. E. Cardinalibus, etiam quacumque natalium seu praecellentium aliarum dignitatum praerogativa insignitis, quod, solo nomine Cardinalis absque ullo saecularis dignitatis additamento contenti, non aliis titulis nuncupentur nec uti inter eos possint, quam eminentissimi et reverendissimi, nec non Eminentiae Reverendissimae, non obstantibus quibuscumque in contrarium facientibus; insuper ut Sanctissimus D. N. dignetur mandare, ut omnes S. R. E. Cardinales, supra recensiti ad unitatem et aequalitatem ordinis construendam, iubeant e propriis sigillis et insignibus quibuscumque, vulgo armis nuncupatis, amoveri coronas, signa ac omnes notas saeculares præter eas, quibus intra scutum armorum eorum familiae tamquam de essentia et integritate eorundem armorum utuntur, et ut in posterum ab illorum usu abstineant, solo pileo, de pretioso Christi sanguine rubente, insigniti ac decorati; ac ulterius Sanctissimus D. N. inhibeat sub poena excommunicationis latae sententiae ac aliis arbitrii sui poenis sculptoribus, pictoribus, ac aliis quibuscumque, ne praedictas notas saeculares in sigillis et armis, aliisque insigniis S. R. E. Cardinalium sculpere ac pingere ac sculpi vel pingi mandare audeant.

Quod quidem decretum praedictus Aloysius Cardinalis retulit supradictam Congregationem censuisse etiam nomine totius Sacri Collegii in praesenti Consistorio Nostro praeferri, ut non solum illud comprobare, verum etiam pro ipsius usu et observantia inviolabili litteras apostolicas cum plumbo expediri iubere dignaremur; quas postea, Cardinales iam promoti qui in Urbe sunt infra decem dies, qui extra illam et in Italia degunt, infra quatuor menses proximos iurare teneantur . . . motu proprio et certa scientia et matura deliberatione . . . perpetuo confirmamus . . . ad quos spectat et spectabit quomodolibet in futurum, sub poenis in eodem decreto contentis, inviolabiliter observari praecipimus et mandamus . . . nunquam censeri praesenti constitutioni derogatum, nec illi in aliquo praeiudicatum, nisi fuerit expresse et dispositive illi, toto eius tenore, derogatum.

D.2.   *Alexander VII.*, 27 Sept. 1659, Decretum circa usum pontificalium Praelatis Episcopo inferioribus concessorum a S. Rituum Congregatione habita coram Ssmo D. N. Alexandro VII. emanatum, Decreta authentica, I, 232--234, n. 1131 (2003).

The decree is laying down 21 rules against abuses :

8. Mitram pretiosam, nisi illis expresse a S. Sede indultam, non adhibeant. Sub mitra pileolum nigri tantum coloris induant. Baculum pastoralem velo albo appenso deferant; ab iisque et alliis pontificalibus etiam de Ordinariorum licentia extra Ecclesias sibi subjectas prorsus abstineant . . .

D.3.   a) 20 Jul. 1660, Declaratio decreti Alexandri VII. de Praelatis Episcopo inferioribus 27 Sept. 1659 C. S. Rituum pro Congregatione Cassinensium, Descreta authentica, I, 240 s., n. 1163 (2056), Congregationi Cassinensium.

ad n. 8. quo usus mitrae pretiosae et baculi sine velo appenso vetitus est, asserentibus monachis, mitram pretiosam ipsis de iure competere, velum quoque numquam eos consuevisse, baculo appensum adhibere, nec esse de ritibus Romanae Ecclesiae sed Ambrosianae tantum : S. R. C. censuit : quoad mitram servandum esse dispositionem cap. 117 Apostolicae De privilegiis in 6°, quoad baculum vero servandum esse Decretum.

b) Sexti Decretalium Lib. V. Tit. VII, De privilegiis, Cap. VI, "Ut Apostolicae Sedis", Clemens IV. (1265—68); Friedberg II, 1086 s.

De fratrum nostrorum consilio praesenti decreto statuimus ut abbates et provincialibus conciliis et episcopalibus synodis, quibus nonnulli eorum interesse tenentur, mitris tantummodo aurifrisiastis (non tamen aureas vel argenteas laminas aut gemmas habentibus), uti possint, non exempti vero simplicibus et albis ac planis utuntur; in aliis vero locis et non exemptis mitris liceat illis uti, prout concessa eis ab eadem S. Sede indulta permittunt.

D.4.   14 Jun. 1687, Decr. Auth. Congr. S. Rituum, I, 383, n. 1782 (3138) Cremonen.

In reply to a complaint of the bishop of Cremona against the provosts of St. Agatha in Cremona & of Pizzighettone the Sacred Congregation of Rites decides :

4. . . . non posse uti mitra pretiosa, et teneri baculum cooperire velo albo.

D.5.   *Benedictus XIV.*, Feb. 1744, Const. "Simul ac", BRC, I, 345 s., Capitulo Cathedralis Ecclesiae Patavinae indulta et privilegia conceduntur :

. . . Pileum itidem gerant ornatum purpureo torulo, honoraria scil. rubri coloris fasciola. Insigni praeterea Familiae suae Protonotarium galerum imponant.

D.6.   *Benedictus XIV.*, 29 Jan. 1752, Decr. auth., II, 101 s., n. 2418 (4224). Ad removendos nonnullos abusus in Eccl. Metrop. Urbinat. circa usum pontificalium aliarumque praerogativarum exercitium, quas dignitates et canonici ultra pontificii Brevis S. M. Benedicti XIII. limitationem sibi indebite arrogabant, hodiernus Archiepiscopus . . .

12. An in insignibus et armis suae familiae appositis vel apponendis in paramentis sacris aliisve rebus Ecclesiam concernentibus, loco mitrae vel una cum ipsa pileum apponere valeant?

ad 12 : negative nisi pro mitra tantum et amplius.

D.7. *Benedictus XIV.*, 17 Feb. 1752, Bulla "In throno iustitiae", BRC, III, I, 343. S. Congr. Rituum. Decreta super modo utendi indulto pontificalium Capitulo et Canonicis Ecclesiae Archiepiscopalis Urbinaten. olim a Sede Apostolica concesso approbantur et confirmantur.

Dubium 12. . . . in eorum armis et insigniis, mitram apponi facere et addere etiam valerent? — Resp. ad 12 : Affirmative quoad mitram tantum.

D.8. *Pius VI.*, 22 Jan. 1796, "Inest profecto", BRC, VI, II, 2916. Ampliatio concessionis factae Capitulo Ecclesiae Metropolitanae Caesenatensis super usum mitrae.

(In 1795 the use of the mitre was granted to the members of the chapter of Cesena. Its heraldic use was not mentioned, cf. BRC, VI, II, 2838. Now it is explicitly granted :) . . . § 3 . . . singuli vestrum vestrique successores mitra simplici ex tela linea, praesente etiam S. R. E. Cardinali . . . auctoritate Apostolica tenore praesentium perpetuo concedimus et indulgemus. . . Insuper vobis vestrumque successoribus ut in propriis armis et insigniis mitram sine pileo apponi facere, et addere possitis, licentiam impertimur. . .

D.9. *Pius VII*, 28 Jul. 1818, "Romanorum Pontificum", BRC, VII, II, 1832 s. Concessio usus mitrae albae pro dignitatibus et canonicis Ecclesiae Cathedralis Liparensis.

§ 3. . . . mitra alba uti libere ac licite possint . . . eisdemque in suis armis, seu insigniis gentilitiis mitram apponi faciendi, et addendi licentiam perpetuo tribuimus. . .

D.10. *Pius VII.*, 13 Dec. 1818, Const. "Cum innumeri" Decr. auth., II, 173-177, n. 2583 (4545).
De privilegiis Protonoteriorum titularium seu honorariorum :

1. . . . uti habitu praelatitio videlicet veste talari et palliolo (mantelletta) nigri coloris.

3. . . . usus collaris et caligarum coloris violacei omnino interdicitur, item et vitta, seu cordula in pileo violacei seu etiam, quo nonnullorum audacia erupit, rosacei aut rubei, quae nigri dumtaxat coloris esse potuerint : eiusdum coloris sit pariter pileum cum lemniscis stemmatibus imponendum.

D.11. Congr. S. Rituum, 27 Aug. 1822, Decr. Auth., II, 202-205, n. 2624 (4593). Baren.

4. Dignitates, Canonici . . . prohibentur . . . ornatum aliquem pontificalem induere absque speciali Apostolicae Sedis privilegio.

5. Quodcumque privilegium ad augendum insignium quarumdam Ecclesiarum splendorem ab Apostolica Sede Dignitatibus, Canonicis, Rectoribus . . . concessum, utpote laesivum dignitati Episcopali, de iure strictissime est interpretandum. Quamobrem nil aliud concessum . . . neque ex indulto alterove privilegio trahi protest consequentia ad alia, quae singulatim descripta non fuerint.

8. . . . mitra simplex ex tela alba cum sericis laciniis rubei coloris.

27. In insigniis seu stemmatibus familiae mitra non apponantur, nisi solo in casu quo expresse concessum sit in literis Apostolicis.

D.12. *Pius VII.*, quarto nonas Julii 1823, Const. "Decet Romanos Pontifices", BRC, VII, II, 2337.

Confirmatio decreti S. R. C. super declaratione privilegiorum circa usum insignium pontificalium, quibus ex Sedis Apostolicae indulto nonnullae dignitates gaudent...

Sapienti proinde consilio praedecessoribus Nostris visum est . . . opportune praefinire, quidnam iuris inducat mitrae ac pontificalium usus, aliaque id genus insignia, quibus placuit Apostolicae Sedi Abbates, Praelatosque nonnullos Episcopo inferiores, et quaedam Canonicorum Collegia honestare...

VII. Sub generico ornamentorum pontificalium nomine, quae ex privilegio . . . insignibus Capitulis . . . conceduntur, intelliguntur; . . . mitra simplex ex tela alba cum sericis laciniis rubei coloris...

XXVII. Insigniis seu stemmatibus familiae mitra non apponatur, nisi solo in casu, quo expresse concessum sit in literis Apostolicis.

D.13. Decreta S. Congr. Caeremonialis habitae die 9 Feb. 1832.

Quum in S. Congr. Caeremoniali quaedam fuerint proposita, quae non multo abhinc tempore inducta Ejus animadversionem postulare videbantur, inter quae id erat, quod nonnumquam rubris lemniscis, vulgo *Fiocchi*, quibus ornantur equi Emmorum Patrum currus vehentes, alii etiam colores inserti reperiantur; et leminscorum numerus in Insignibus difformiter auctus interdum deprehendatur : itemque illud, quod nonnulli Cappellae Pontificiae Inservientes indebitis utantur vestibus; et praedictorum Emmorum Caudatarii aliquid in habitu eorum proprio immutaverint : eadem S. Congr. ad uniformitatem debitam restituendam, et abusus eliminandos enunciatis die et mense haec decrevit.

. . . Lemniscorum, qui circum Insignia Emmorum Patrum collocantur, numerus ad quindecim utrimque non multis ab hinc annis evectus retineri valeat, majore quolibet numero omnibus interdicto.

. . . Facta autem SSmo Domino Nostro *Gregorio PP. XVI* per me infrascriptum Secretarium de praemissis omnibus relatione, idem SSmus Dominus Noster praefata Decreta non solum approbavit, sed inviolabiliter ab omnibus et singulis, ad quos ea spectant, servari praecepit. Hac die 14 Aprilis 1832 SSmi Domini Nostri Pontificatus anno secundo.

B. Episc. Ostien et Veliternen. Card. Pacca S. C. Dec. Praef.

Josephus De Ligne, Secretarius.

D.14. Congr. S. Rituum, 27 Feb. 1847, Decr. auth., II, 343 s., n. 2930 (5065). Beneventana

1. An Abbas memoratae Collegiatae, gaudens usu mitrae, baculi pastoralis aliorumque pontificalium insignium, uti possit mitra auriphrygiata et baculo episcopali, vel potius alterius formae et ab episcopali distinctis?

Ad. 1. Negative, sed mitra tantum ex tela simplici, et baculo Abbatiali cum velo.

D.15. *Pius X.*, 21 Feb. 1905, *Motu Proprio* "Inter multiplices curas". Decr. auth., VII, n. 4154; et : SSmi D. N. P I I *Papae X Motu Proprio* De Protonotariis Apostolicis, Praelatis Urbanis, et aliis qui nonnullis privilegiis Praelatorum propriis fruuntur. Typis polyglottis Vaticanis 1942.

Inter multiplices curas, quibus ob officium Nostrum apostolicum premimur, illa etiam imponitur, ut venerabilium Fratrorum Nostrorum, qui episcopali charactere praefulgent, pontificales praerogativas, uti par est, tueamur...

157

Ex quo praesertim Pontificalium usus per Decessores Nostros Romanos Pontifices aliquibus Praelatis, Episcopali charactere non insignitis, concessus est, id saepe accidit, ut, vel malo hominum ingenio, vel prava aut lata nimis interpretatione, ecclesiastica disciplina haud leve detrimentum ceperit, et episcopalis dignitas non parum iniuriae . . .

Hisce tamen neglectis, vel ambitioso conatu, facili aufugio, amplificatis, hac nostra aetate saepe videre est Praelatos, immoderato insignium et praerogativarum usu, praesertim circa Pontificalia, viliores reddere dignitatem et honorem eorum, qui sunt revera Pontifices. . .

A) De Protonotariis Apostolicis.

I — De Protonotariis Apostolicis de numero Participantium.

. . . 3. Protonot. Ap. de num. Part. habitu praelatitio rite utuntur, et alio quem vocant *pianum*, atque insignibus prout infra numeris 16, 17, 18 describuntur.

. . . 5. Quod vero circa usum Pontificalium insignium Xystus V in sua Constitutione "Laudabilis Sedis Apostolicae sollicitudo" . . . Protonotariis Participantibus concessit "Mitra et quibuscumque aliis Pontificalibus insignibus . . .'

6. In Pontificalibus peragendis semper eis inhibatur usus throni, pastoralis baculi et cappae; . . .

II — De Protonotariis Apostolicis Supranumerariis.

13. Ad hunc Protonotariorum ordinem nemo tamquam privatus aggregabitur, sed iis tantum aditus fiet, qui Canonicatu potiuntur in tribus Capitulis Urbis Patriarchalium, . . . itemque iis qui Dignitate aut Canonicatu potiuntur in Capitulis aliarum quarumdam extra Urbem ecclesiarum quibus privilegia Protonotariorum *de numero* Apostolica Sedes concesserit, ubique fruenda . . .

16. Habitum praelatitium gestare valent coloris violacei, in sacris functionibus, . . . pileum item nigrum cum vitta serica, . . . eiusdem rubini coloris . . .

17. Alio autem habitu uti poterunt, Praelatorum proprio, vulgo *piano*, in Congregationibus, conventibus, solemnibus audientiis ecclesiasticis et civilibus, . . ac pileo nigro cum chordulis et sericis floculis rubini coloris. Communi habitu incedentes, caligas et collare violacei coloris ac pileum gestare poterunt, ut supra dicitur.

18. Propriis insignibus seu stemmatibus imponere poterunt pileum cum lemniscis ac flocculis duodecim, sex hinc, sex inde pendentibus eiusdem *rubini* coloris, sine Cruce vel Mitra.

. . . 34. . . . Verum, cum eadem collective coetui Canonicorum conferantur, Canonici ipsi, tamquam, singuli, iis uti nequibunt, nisi Praelati Urbani fuerint nominati et antea suae ad Canonicatum vel Dignitatem promotionis et auspicatae iam possessionis, atque inter Praelatos aggregationis, ut in n 14 dicitur, testimonium Conlegio Protonotariorum Patricipantium exhibuerint; coram ipsius Conlegii Decano, vel per se vel per legitimum procuratorem, Fidei professionem et fidelitatis jusjurandum de more praestiterint, ac de his postea, exhibito documento, proprium Ordinarium certiorem fecerint.

III — De Protonotariis Apostolicis ad instar Participantium.

42. Inter Protonotarios Apostolicos ad instar Participantium illi viri ecclesiastici adnumerantur, quibus Ap. Sedes hunc horonem conferre voluerit, ac praeterea Dignitates et Canonici alicuius Capituli praestantioris, quibus conlegialiter titulus et

privilegia Protonotariorum, cum addito "ad instar", ubique utenda, fuerint ab eadem Ap. Sede collata . . .

45. Quod pertinet ad habitum praelatitium, *pianum* et communem, stemmata et choralia insignia, habitum et locum in Pontificia Cappella, omnia observabunt, uti supra dictum est de Protonotariis Supranumerariis, nn. 16, 17, 18, 19, 20.

IV — De Protonotariis Apostolicis Titularibus seu Honorariis.

59. Cum Ap. Sedes non sibi uni jus reservaverit Protonotarios Titulares seu Honorarios nominandi, sed Nuntiis Apostolicis, Conlegio Protonotariorum Partic. et forte aliis jamdiu delegaverit, . . . leges seu conditiones renovare placet, quibus rite honesteque ad ejusmodi dignitatem quilibet candidatus valeat evehi, juxta Pii Pp. VII . . . Constitutionem "Cum innumeri" . . .

60. . . . constet indubie : 1° de honesta familiae conditione; 2° de aetate saltem annorum quinque et viginti; 3° de statu clericali et caelibe; 4° de Laurea doctoris in utroque aut canonico tantum jure, vel in Theologia, vel in S. Scriptura; 5° de morum honestate et gravitate, ac de bona apud omnes aestimatione; 6° de non communibus in Ecclesiae bonum promovendum laudibus comparatis; 7° de idoneitate ad Protonotariatum cum decore sustinendum, habita etiam annui census ratione, juxta regionis uniuscuiusque aestimationem.

61. Quod si huiusmodi Protonotariatus honor alicui Canonicorum coetui ab Ap. Sede conferatur (. . .), eo ipso, quo quis Dignitatem aut Canonicatum est legitime consecutus, Protonotarius nuncupabitur.

62. Pariter, qui Vicarii Generalis aut etiam Capitularis munere fungitur, hoc munere dumtaxat perdurante, erit Protonotarius Titularis : hinc, si Dignitate aut Canonicatu in Cathedrali non gaudeat, quando choro interesse velit, habitu Protonotarii praelatitio, qui infra describitur, jure utetur.

63. Protonotarii Apost. Tit. sunt Praelati extra Urbem, . . . Praelatorum Domus Pontificiae honoribus non gaudent, neque inter Summi Pontificis Familiares adnumerantur.

64. . . . rite utuntur habitu praelatitio, nigri ex integro coloris . . .

67. . . . gestare poterunt, cum pileo chordula ac floccis nigris ornato.

68. Propriis insignibus seu stemmatibus, pileum imponere valeant, sed nigrum tantummodo, cum lemniscis et sex hinc et sex inde flocculis pendentibus, item ex integro nigris.

. . . 74. Denique qui Protonotariatu Apostolico Honorario donati sunt tamquam privatae personae, titulo, honoribus et privilegiis Protonotariatus uti nequeunt, nisi antea diploma suae nominationis Conlegio Protonotariorum Participantium exhibuerint, fideique Professionem ac fidelitatis juramentum coram Ordinario, aut alio viro in ecclesiastica dignitate constituto, emiserint. Qui vero ob Canonicatum, Dignitatem aut Vicariatum, Protonotarii titulo potiti fuerint, nisi jusjurandum praestiterint, memoratis honoribus et privilegiis, quae superius recensentur, tantummodo intra propriae diocesis limites uti poterunt.

75. Qui secus agere, aliisque, praeter descripta, privilegiis uti praesumpserint, si ab Ordinario semel et bis admoniti non paruerint, eo ipso honore et juribus Protonotarii privatos se sciant; . . .

76. Vicarii Generales vel Capitulares, itemque Dignitates et Canonici, nomine atque honoribus Protonotariatus titularis gaudentes, si quavis ex causa, a munere,

Dignitate aut Canonicatu cessent, eo ipso, titulo, honoribus et juribus ipsius Protonotariatus excident.

B) De ceteris Praelatis Romanae Curiae.

. . . 79. Hi autem habitum, sive quem vocant *pianum*, gestare poterunt, juxta Romanae Curiae consuetudinem, prout supra describitur nn. 16, 17; numquam . . . alio uti colore quam violaceo, in bireti floccolo et pilei vitta, opere reticulato distincta, sive chordulis et flocculis, etiam in pileo stemmatibus imponendo ut n. 18 dictum est, nisi, pro eorum aliquo, constet de majori privilegio.

C) De Dignitatibus, Canonicis et aliis, qui nonnullis privilegiis Praelatorum propriis fruuntur.

80. Ex Romanorum Pontificium indulgentia, insignia quaedam praelatitia aut pontificalia aliis Conlegiis, praesertim Canonicorum, eorumve Dignitatibus, quocumque nomine nuncupentur, vel a priscis temporibus tribui consueverunt; cum autem ejusmodi privilegia deminutionem quamdam episcopali dignitati videantur afferre, idcirco ea sunt de jure strictissime interpretanda . . .

D.16. S. Congr. Consistorialis Decretum de vetitis nobilitatis familiaris titulis et signis in Episcoporum inscriptionibus et armis. 15 Jan. 1915. A. A. S., 7, 172.
Apostolica Constitutione cuius initium "Militantis Ecclesiae" die 19 dec. 1644 data, S. Pont. Innocentius X. mandavit ut "omnes S. R. E. Cardinales ad unitatem et aequalitatem ordinis construendam, iubeant e propriis sigillis et insignibus quibuscumque, vulgo armis nuncupatis, amoveri coronas, signa ac omnes notas saeculares, praeter eas quibus intra scutum armorum eorum familiae tamquam de essentia et integritate eorumdem armorum utuntur, et ut in posterum ab illorum usu abstineant".

Ad unam vero eademque rationem hac in re etiam quoad Episcopos indicendam Ssmus D. N. Benedictus PP XV legem, quae supra relata est, ad eos extendendum opportunum censuit. Quapropter Sanctitas Sua hoc edi iussit consistoriale decretum, quo Patriarchae, Archiepiscopi et Episcopi omnes tam residentiales quam titulares in posterum in suis sigillis et insignibus seu armis, itemque in edictorum inscriptionibus, titulos nobiliares, coronas, quae nobilitatem propriae familiae vel gentis ostendant, addere penitus prohibentur, nisi forte dignitas aliqua saecularis ipsi episcopali aut archiepiscopali sedi sit adnexa; aut nisi agatur de Ordine equestri S. Joannis Hierosolymitani aut S. Sepulchri. Contrariis non obstantibus quibusvis. Datum Romae ex Secretaria S. C. Constistorialis, die 15 Jan. 1915.

C. Card. De Lai, Eps. Sabinen.,
Secretarius.
Fr. Thomas Boggiani, Adsessor.

D.17. *Pius XI.*, 15 Aug. 1934, Constitutio Apostolica "Ad incrementum decoris".
A. A. S., 26, 497.
De quibusdam Praelatis Romanae Curiae et variis eorum ordinibus.

I. Inter Praelatos Romanae Curiae post Praelatos "di fiocchetti" nuncupatos primum locum immediate obtinent ratione muneris Excellentissimi Praelati qui in sacris Romanis Congregationibus Assessoris vel Secretarii munere funguntur, etsi charactere episcopali careant. . .

II. Vera autem Praelatorum Collegia apud Curiam quattuor numerantur, quae iuxta ordinem praecedentiae hic describuntur, nimirum :

1. Collegium Protonotariorum Apostolicorum de numero Participantium;

2. Collegium Praelatorum Auditorum S. Rom. Rotae;

3. Collegium Clericorum Rev. Camerae Apostolicae;

4. Collegium Praelatorum Votantium Signaturae Apostolicae, cui quidem Collegio adiiciuntur, quamquam verum et proprium Collegium non constituant, Praelati Referendarii eiusdem Signaturae Apostolicae.

V. Sodales emeriti Collegiorum Praelatorum de quibus agitur numeris XXVIII, XXXII, CVI et CXXX, modo ad dignitatem superiorem promoti non fuerint, subsequuntur immediate proprii Collegii membra ordinaria, . . .

VII. Habitus Praelatitius, vulgo "di formalità", seu in sacris functionibus adhibendus ab omnibus Praelatis Romanae Curiae, de quibus in praesenti Constitutione, sive pertinent ad Collegia praefata, sive non pertinent, ille est, quo utuntur Praelati Domestici quique constat . . . pileo item nigro, circumdetur chordula violacea cum flocculis eiusdemque coloris . . .
Protonotarii Apostolici utuntur . . . pileo cum chordulis item rubini coloris.

XVII. Singuli Assessores et Secretarii SS. Congregationum omnibus juribus et privilegiis Protonotariorum Apostolicorum de numero Participantium . . . gaudent ad personam durante munere, etiamsi horum Collegio non adscribantur.

XIX. Praecedentiae gradum supra alios Praelatos infra Praelatos vulgo "di fiocchetti" constitutos, etiam episcopali seu archiepiscopali dignitate fulgentes, salvo jure Metropolitae vel Ordinarii loci in suo territorio, habebunt ubique, etiam singuli . . .

XX. His privilegiis fruuntur tantummodo durante munere; deposito vero munere, nisi ad cardinalatum vel aliam dignitatem assumantur quae cum Protonotarii dignitate componi nequeat, aut nisi aliud expresse caveatur, statim, ipso jure Protonotarii ad instar fiunt, cum omnibus juribus et privilegiis huic dignitati adnexis.

XXI. Omnia quae de Assessoribus et Secretariis SS. Congregationum Romanarum in hoc capite dicuntur . . . dicta etiam intelligantur de . . . Magistro seu Praefecto cubiculi Summi Pontificis, Secretario Tribunalis Signaturae Apostolicae, Decano S. Rom. Rotae, Substituto Secretariae Status.

XXVIII. Si quis Protonotarius de numero Participantium post decem annos a sua cooptatione Collegium relinquit, per novum quinquennium eiusdem privilegiis fruitur : dein, ipso iure, fit Protonotarius ad instar. Quodsi ante decennium e Collegio discedat, statim, ipso iure, fit Protonotarius ad instar . . . Si vero aliquando, ex gratia Pontificia, Protonotarius Participans aliquis declaretur emeritus, is omnibus privilegiis honorificis Collegii frui poterit, iuxta n. V.

XXX. Eadem insignia et privilegia sed durante munere et in proprio territorio tantum habent etiam Vicarii Apostolici et Praefecti Apostolici, nec non Administratores Apostolici diocesibus ad tempus dati.

LIV. Protonotarii supranumeraii sunt ii qui canonicatu potiuntur in Basilicis Patriarchalibus Urbis scil. Lateranensi, Vaticana, Liberiana, modo Litteras Apostolicas in forma brevi acceperint et iusjurandum emiserint. Item Canonici quarumdam aliarum Ecclesiarum extra Urbem. Priores tamen titulo praefato insigniti erunt ad vitam, posteriores vero durante munere.

LV. Munera, jura, privilegiaque Protonotariorum supranumerariorum ea erunt quae descripta sunt in Litteris Apostolicis a Pio X motu proprio datis, "Inter multiplices" sub numeris 13-41, 80.

LVI. Protonotarii ad instar praeter iis de quibus in XX et XXVIII ii erunt, quos Summus Pontifex hac dignitate insigniverit, nec non qui Canonicatu in quibusdam determinatis Capitulis potiuntur. Priores erunt Protonotarii ad vitam, posteriores vero durante munere. Quod si posteriores nominati fuerint Praelati Domestici ut personae privatae subiecti erunt dispositionibus contentis in Apostolicis Litteris a Pio X motu proprio datis "Inter multiplices", nn. 43, 50, 58.

LXXI. Statim a sua nominatione Auditores ipso facto fiunt Praelati Domestici et Familiares Summi Pontificis et hanc dignitatem retinent quandiu munere Auditorum funguntur vel cum emeriti declarentur.

LXXIII. Gaudent iure Pontificalium eodem modo atque de Protonotariis Apostolicis de numero Participantium dicutm est supra, n. XLIII.

LXXXII. Ex Auditoribus qui emeriti declarati fuerint, iisdem fruuntur privilegiis ac ordinarii Auditores, cum ea limitatione tantum quae in numero V describitur.

LXXXVI. Collegium Clericorum Rev. Camerae Apostolicae constat octo Praelatis quorum antiquior, ad normam numeri IV, titulum assumit decani.

CV. Clerici Camerae eo ipso sunt Praelati Domestici et Familiares S. Pontificis, horumque proptera gaudent privilegiis.

CXVI. Si Clerici Rev. Cam. Ap. declarati fuerint emeriti, munera quidem aliroum Clericorum Camerae non praestant amplius, privilegiis vero eorum frui perseverant, salvo praescripto numeri V.

CXVIII. Praelati Votantes Signaturae Apostolicae constituunt verum propriumque Collegium : hoc autem constant novem sodalibus . . . qui omnes . . . inter Praelatos referendarios eligendi sunt . . .

CXXX. Ex Praelatis Votantibus qui emeriti declarati fuerint, iisdem fruuntur privilegiis ac Votantes ordinarii . . .

CXXXIII. Praelati Referendarii verum et proprium Collegium non constituunt.

CXLII. Referendarii dignitas secumfert dignitates et privilegia Praelati Domestici et Familiaris S. Pontificis.

. . . Non obstantibus, quatenus opus sit, cann. 4, 10, 70 ss. 102 § 2 Codicis I. C.

D.18. Formula juramenti a novis Cardinalibus praestandi :
   a) Constitutiones Apostolicae et decreta quae jurantur ac furmula juramenti praestari solita a S. R. E. Cardinalibus dum ad Cardinalatum promoventur. Urbini 1738.
   Ego N. . . . S. R. E. Cardinalis N. . . . promitto, et juro, me ab hac hora deinceps, quamdiu vixero, fidelem et obedientem beato Petro, Sanctaeque Apostolicae Romanae Ecclesiae ac Sanctissimo D. N. . . . Papae . . . eiusque Successoribus . . . et singula decreta a S. Caeremoniali Congregatione hactenus emanata, et in posterum emanatura pro sublimi Cardinalatus honore, et dignitate servanda, decerni, statui, et ordinari contigerit, et signanter Motum Proprium eiusdem *Innocentii* Papae X, confirmantis decreti ab eadem S. Caeremoniali Congregatione facti super aequalitate inter S. R. E. Cardinales servanda in honorificis appellationibus, seu titulis eorum cuilibet attribuendis, et super expunctione coronarum, aliarumque notarum saecularium e gentilitiis eorundem Cardinalium insigniis, seu armis, sub datum Romae apud S. Petrum anno Incarnationis Dominicae millesimo sexcentesimo quadragesimo quarto, decimo quarto Kal. Januarii, . . . iuxta illius tenorem mihi plene cognitum,

me ad unguem observaturum, neque quidquam, quod eiusdem Cardinalatus honori, et dignitati quovis modo, et ex quavis causa repugnet, aut diminuat, acturum...

b) Formula juramentia novis Cardinalibus praestandi, Typis polyglottis Vaticanis, 1946.

Ego . . . Sanctae Romanae Ecclesiae Cardinalis . . . promitto et iuro . . . Item omnia et singula Decreta, praesertim a S. Congregatione Caeremoniali hactenus emantata, et in posterum emananda, pro sublimi Cardinalatus honore et dignitate conservanda, ad unguem observaturum, neque quidquam, quod eiusdem Cardinalatus honori et dignitati quovis modo et ex quavis causa repugnet, aut diminuat, acturum...

D.19. *Pius XII.*, 12 Maii 1951. S. C. Consistorialis Decretum
De vetito civilium nobiliarium titulorum usu in episcoporum inscriptionibus et armis.

Attentis dispositionibus, quae de nobilitatis familiaris titulorum et signorum usu in Episcoporum inscriptionibus et armis iamdiu latae fuerunt, i.e. Constitutione Apostolica "Militantis Ecclesiae" diei 19 decembris 1644 et Consistoriali Decreto diei 15 ianuarii 1915, (v. *Acta Ap. Sedis*, a. VII-1915, pag. 172), Ssmus Dominus Noster Pius Divina Providentia PP. XII, mature perpendense huiusmodi saeculares nobilitatis titulos vel notas pristinum amisisse iuridicum fundamentum et ab hodiernis rerum hominumque condicionibus dissentier, veteres immutare novasque edicere normas peropportunum duxit.

Quapropter, praesenti Consistoriali Decreto, idem Ssmus Dominus Noster decernere dignatus est ut Ordinarii omnes in suis sigillis et insignibus seu armis, necnon in epistularum ac edictorum inscriptionibus, titulorum nobiliarium, coronarum aliarumve saecularium notarum usu in posterum prorsus abstineant, etiam si ipsi episcopali vel archiepiscopali sedi sint adnexa.

Contrariis quibusvis, etiam specialissima mentione dignis, minime obstantibus.

Datum Romae, ex Aedibus S. Congregationis Consistorialis, die 12 Maii 1951.

✠ Fr. A. I. Card. Piazza, Ep. Sabinen, et Mandelen., *a Secretis.*

Iosephus Ferretto, *Adsessor.*

D.20. *Paulus VI.*, 31 Martii 1969. Secretaria status seu papalis
Instructio : Circa vestes, titulos et insignia generis Cardinalium, Episcoporum et Praelatorum ordine minorum.

Ut sive sollicite suum munus tueretur universae vigilandi Ecclesiae, sive Concilii Oecumenici Vaticani II indicia et consilia ad effectum adduceret, Summus Pontifex Paulus VI nihil praetermisit, quin considerationem suam etiam in quasdam vitae ecclesiasticae externas formas intenderet, ut pariter eas magis ad mutata temporum adiuncta componeret, pariter aptius ad summa animorum bona referret, quae iis formis et significari et foveri oportet.

De re videlicet agitur, qua mens hominum, qui nunc sunt, in primis commovetur, et in qua, extremis utriusque vitatis appetitionibus, proprietas et dignitas accommodentur opus est ad simplicitatem, ad utilitatem, ad demissionis denique et paupertatis spiritum, quo eos praesertim ornari decet, qui, cum ecclesiasticis officiis initiati sint, certum onus idcirco receperunt operam populo Dei navandi.

28. Sive Patribus Cardinalibus, sive Episcopis conceditur, ut generis insigne adhibere possint.

Huius vero insignis aspectus ad normam artis exarandorum insignium delineandus erit, idemque simplex atque perspicuus sit oportet. Ab huiusmodi autem insigni sive baculi pastorali sive infulae effigies tollantur.

29. Patribus Cardinalibus permittitur, ut proprium insigne in templi fronte, quod eorum Titulum vel Diaconiam efficiat, depictum suspendere curent.

Datum ex Aedibus Vaticanis, die XXXI mensis Martii, anno MCMLXIX.

HAMLETUS I. Card. CICOGNANI
a publicis Ecclesiae negotiis

BIBLIOGRAPHY

A. Sources

Acta Apostolicae Sedis (A. A. S.), Commentarium officiale, Typis polyglottis Vaticanis, 1909-1969, Vol. I-LXI.

Acta Gregorii Papae XVI recensita et digesta cura ac studio A. M. Bernasconi, Romae, 1901-1904, I-IV.

Acta Leonis XIII P. M., Romae, 1881-1905, I-XXIV.

Acta Pii IX P. M., Romae, 1854-1865, I-IX.

Acta Sanctae Sedis, Romae, 1865-1908, I-XLI.

Annuario Pontificio, Vaticano, 1943, 1944, 1945, 1946, 1947, 1948, 1951, 1969.

Bizzarri, A., Collectanea in usum Secreteriae S. Congregationis Episcoporum et Regularium, Romae, 1863 et 1885.

Bullarii Romani Continuatio (B. R. C.), Prati, 1840-49, IV/1-VI/3.

Bullarium Benedicti XIV P. O. M., olim Prosperi Card. de Lambertinis (B. R. C.), Prati, 1845-47, I-III/2.

Bullarium Romanum, Magnum (B. R.), Bullarum, Diplomatum et Privilegiorum Rom. Pontificum Taurinensis Editio, Augustae Taurinorum et Neapoli 1857-1872, I-XXIV; Appendix, Augustae Taurinorum 1867.

Caeremoniale Episcoporum (C. E.), cura et studio Josephi Catalani, Paris, 1860, I-II.

Caeremoniale Episcoporum Clementis VIII, Innocentii X et Benedicti XIII, jussu editum, Benedicti XIV et Leonis XIII auctoritate recognitum, Editio I post typicam, Augustae Taurinorum, 1893.

Decreta Authentica Congregationis Sacrorum Rituum, Romae, 1898-1927, I-V, I-II.

Mansi, Joannes Dominicus, Sacrorum Conciliorum nova et amplissima collectio, Reproduction en facimilé, Paris-Leipzig, 1901-1927, I-LIII.

Pius X, Motu proprio "Inter multiplices curas" Typis polyglottis Vaticanis, 1942.

Pontificale Romanum (P. R.) Clementis VIII ac Urbani VII, cura et studio Iosephi Catalani, Parisiis, 1850, I-III.

B. Canon Law

Andreucci, Andrea Girolamo, S. J., Hierarchia ecclesiastica, Romae, 1766, I-II.

Barbosa, Augustinus, Summa Apostolicarum Decisionum extra ius commune vagantium, Genevae, 1650.

Tractatus de Canonicis et Dignitatibus, Lugduni, 1668.

Bernardus de Pavia, Summa decretalium. Regensburg, 1860.

Bouix, D., Tractatus de Curia Romana, Paris, 1880. *Tractatus de Episcopo*, Paris 1889³, I-II.

Cappello. Felix M., Summa iuris canonici, Romae I⁴ 1945, II³ 1939, III² 1940.

Codex Iuris Canonici (C. I. C.) Pii X P. M. iussu digestus Benedicti XV auctoritate promulgatus praefatione, fontium annotatione et indice analytico- alphabatico ab Emmo Petro Card. Casparri auctus Romae, 1917, ed. 1943.

Cohellius, Jacobus, Notitia Cardinalatus, in qua nedum de S. R. E. Cardinalium origine, dignitate, praeminentia et privilegiis . . . , Romae 1653

Creusen (Joseph), S. J., Religieux et religieuses, Paris, 1940⁵.

Decretales Gregorii Papae IX suae integritate cum glossis restitutae, Romae 1582.

Durandus, Wilhelm, Speculum iudiciale, Frankfurt a. M. 1668.

Extravagantes tum viginti D. Joannis papae XXII tum communes suae integritati una cum glossis restituate, Romae, 1582.

Ferraris, F. Lucii, Prompta bibliotheca canonica iuridica moralis theologica, Romae 1844-55, I-VII, editio novissima Romae, 1885-92, I-VIII; IX Supplementum, Romae, 1899.

Friedberg, Aemilianus, Corpus Iuris Canonici, Lipsiae, I 1879, II, 1881.

Gaufred de Trani, Summa super rubricis decretalium, Basileae, 1487.

Hofmeister, Philipp, O. S. B., Mitra und Stab der wirklichen Prälaten ohne bischöflichen Charakter, Stutz, Kirchenrechtliche Abhandlungen, Heft 104, Stuttgart, 1928.

Innocentis IV P. M. in quinque Decretalium Libros . . . commentaria doctissima, Venetiis 1570, Francofurti a. M. 1570.

Pennacchi, Josephus (Avanzini Petrus), Commentaria in constitutionem Apostolicae Sedis qua censurae latae sententiae limitantur, Romae, 1883, 1888, I-II.

Petra, Card. Vinc., Commentaria in Constitutiones Apostolicas, Venetiis 1741.

Pignatelli, Jacobi, Consultationes canonicae, Venetiis, 1722-23, I-IV.

Pittorno, Jo. Bapt., Constiutitones Pontificum, Decisiones ad sacros Ritus spectantes, Venetiis, 1730.

Plati, Hieronymus, S. J., De Cardinalis dignitate et officio tractatus, ed. quarta a Joanne Andrea *Tria*, Romae, 1746.

Rotae, S. Romanae, Decisiones recentiores a Prospero Farinaccio selectae, Venetiis 1697-1716, I-XXIV.

Segusia, Henricus de, Summa aurea, Regensburg, 1480.

Tancredus de Bononia, Libri de iudiciorum ordine, edition F. Bergmann, Göttingen, 1842.

Trombetta, Aloysius, De iuribus et privilegiis praelatorum Romanae Curiae tractatus canonico liturgicus, Surrenti, 1906.

Tudeschis, Nicolaus de, Opera, Venetiis, 1617, I-IX.

Van Espen, Zeger Bernardus, Ius canonicum universum, Lovanii, 1753.

Van Haeften, Benedictus, O. S. B., Disquisitorium monasticum libri XII Antwerpiae, 1644.

Vermeersch, A., S. J., De l'admission dans les églises de drapeaux non bénits, Revue d'organisation et de défense religieuse, 1913, 590 ss. Paris, 1913.

Vermeersch, A., S. J., et *Creusen*, J., S. J., Epitome iuris canonici. Mechlinae-Romae, I 1937⁶, II 1934⁵, III 1931⁴.

Wernz, Franc. Xav., S. J., Ius decretalium, Romae-Prati, I, 1913³, II 1915³, III 1908², IV 1911², V 1914, VI 1913.

Wernz-Vidal, Ius canonicum auctore P. Fr. X. Wernz, S. J. ad codicis normam exactum opera P. Petri Vidal, S. J. Romae, 1927-1938, I-VII.

C. Heraldry and Sigillography

Achen, Sven Tito,
   a) Danske kommunevaabner, Copenhagen 1967.
   b) Identifikation af anonyme vaabenskjolde, Copenhagen 1972.
   c) Dansk heraldisk bibliografi, Copenhagen 1971.
   d) Danske adelsvaabner, Copenhagen 1973.
   e) Symboler, Copenhagen 1975.

Almeida-Langhans, F. P., Heraldica ciencia de temas vivos, Lisbon 1966.

Amstutz, W., Japanese Emblems & Designs, Zurich 1970.

Archives Heraldiques Suisses, Neuchâtel, Zurich, Basle, Lausanne 1887-1977.

Armengol y de Pereyrar, Alejandro, Heraldica, Barcelona 1947.

Artin Pacha, Jacoub, Contribution à l'étude du blason en Orient, London 1902.

Barbier de Montault, Mgr Xavier,
   a) Armorial des évêques et administrateurs de l'insigne église d'Angers, Angers 1863.
   b) Des armoiries ecclésiastiques d'après le droit commun, Arras, 1872, et Giornale Araldico 1877/78, 85-98, Pisa, 1878.
   c) Armorial des Papes, Pas-de-Calais, 1877.
   d) La Croix à double croisillon, Montauban, 1882.
   e) Œuvres complètes, Poitiers et Paris, 1889-1899, I-XIV.
   f) La loi des chapeaux ecclésiastiques dans l'art héraldique, Vannes, 1901.

Bartolus de Saxoferrato, Tractatus de insigniis et armis (ca. 1350), dans Johannis Fabri Jurisconsulti Galli, In Justiniani Imperatoris codicem breviarium . . . , 254 ss., Lugduni, 1550; edited also by Hauptmann, Bonn 1883 & Evans, Medieval heraldry, Cardiff, 1945.

Battandier, Mgr Albert, Annuaire pontifical, 1900, 200; 1902, 366 ss.; 1913, 774 s.; 1919, 454 ss.; 1920, 464 ss.; 1922, 429; 1932, 859. Paris, 1899 ss.

Baty, Thomas, Vital heraldry, Edinburgh 1962.

Beatiano, Giulio Cesare de, L'araldo veneto, Venezia 1860.

Beaumont, Albert de, Recherche sur l'origine du blason, Paris, 1853.

Benziger, Dr. Carl, Die kirchl. Heraldik in der Schweiz, Schweizer Rundschau, Einsiedeln, 1916/17, V.

Berchem, Egon Freiherr von, Galbreath, D. L. and *Hupp*, Otto, Beiträge zur Geschichte der Heraldik, Berlin, 1910 & 1939.

Berghman, Arvid, Heraldisk bilderbok, Stockholm 1951.

Bernd, Christian Samuel Theodor,
   a) Allgemeine Schriftenkunde der gesamten Wappenwissenschaft. Bonn, 1835.
   b) Handbuch der Wappenwissenschaft, Leipzig, 1856.

Berry, William,
   a) Encyclopedia heraldica, or complete dictionary of heraldry, London (1828-40) I-III.
   b) *Heraldry*, London.

Blunt, E., The elements of Armoiries, London, 1610.

Bofarull, Francisco de, La heraldica en la filigrana del papel, Barcelona, 1901.

Bossewell, Works of Armoirie, 1572.

Bouly de Lesdain, Claude,
   a) Les brisures d'après les sceaux (extrait des Archives héraldiques suisses) Neuchâtel, 1896.
   b) Les plus anciennes armoiries françaises (1127-1300) (extrait des Archives héraldiques suisses) Neuchâtel, 1897.

c) Les armoiries de femmes d'après les sceaux (extrait de l'Annuaire du Conseil héraldique de France, 1898). Saint-Armand, 1898.

d) Notes sur quelques changements d'armoiries au XIIe et XIIIe siècles, dans Archives héraldiques suisses, 1899, p. 76-82, et 106-116; 1900, p. 1-20 et 44-62.

e) Études héraldiques sur le XIIe siècle, dans l'Annuaire du Conseil héraldique de France, 20e année, 1907, p. 185-244.

Boutell's Heraldry revised by John Brooke-Little, London 1973 & 1978.

Brassard, Br. Gerard, Armorial of the american hierarchy, Worcester, Mass.

Burke, J. B.,
a) Encyclopedia of heraldry, London, 1878.
b) General armory of England, London, 1884.

Cappelen, A. K. T., Norske slektsvapen, Oslo, 1969.

Cascante, J. V., Heraldica general y fuentes de las armas de España, Barcelona, 1974.

Chassant, Alph. et Delbarre, P.-J., Dictionnaire de sigillographie pratique, Paris, 1860.

Chasseneux, Bartelemy de, Catalogus gloriae mundi, Lyon, 1546, Francofurti a. M. 1586, Genève, 1617.

Christyn (Baron de Meerbeek), Jean-Baptiste, Jurisprudentia heroica, Bruxelles, 1668.

Clark, Hugh, An introduction to heraldry, London, 1899. 18th edition, Tabard Press, 1974.

Cole, H., Heraldry and floral forms used in decoration, London, 1922.

Collegio Araldico, Libro d'oro della nobiltà italiana, 1914/15, Roma, 1915. Libro della nobiltà italiana, Roma, 1929 and 1969-72.

Consulta Araldica, Massimario della, Roma, 1905.
— Memoriale della, Roma, 1924.
— Nuovo ordinamento della, Roma, 1896.

Cosson, André Armorial des Cardinaux, Archevêques et Évêques français actuels au 1er janvier 1917, Paris, 1917.

Coulon, Auguste, Éléments de sigillographie ecclésiastique française, Revue d'histoire de l'église de France, XVIII, 30-59, 163-188, 341-368, Paris, 1932.

Courtray, Albert-Marie, Contribution à l'armorial des Papes, Lille, 1908.

Crollalanza, Goffredo di, Enciclopedia araldico-cavalleresca, Pisa 1876-77. Araldica ufficiale, Pisa, 1891.

Cussans, John E., Handbook of Heraldry, London, 1893.

Dahlby, Frithof, Svensk heraldisk uppslagsbok, Stockholm, 1964.

Dansaert, G., L'art héraldique et ses diverses applications, Bruxelles, 1912.

Davenport, C., English heraldic book Stamps, London, 1909.

Dennys, Rodney, The heraldic imagination, London, 1975.

Dubois, Fréd. Th.,
a) Les armoiries des abbés de Saint-Maurice,s évêques de Bethléem, Fribourg, 1908.
b) Armoiries du diocese et des évêques de Lausanne dès 1500, Lausanne, 1910.
c) Les en-têtes armoriés des imprimés officiels des évêques de Lausanne aux XVIe, XVIIe et XVIIIe siècles, Fribourg, 1911.

Dimier A. & M. Cocheril, Les plus beaux Blasons de l'Armorial Cistercien, Collectanea O.Cist S.O. 1956-1959.

Dubrulle, (Henri), Armoiries ecclésiastiques, Grand almanach du monde catholique, Bruges, 1910.

Du Puy Demportes, J.-B., Traité historique et moral du blason, Amsterdam et Berlin, 1754, I-II.

Du Roure de Paulin, Baron, L'Héraldique ecclésiastique, Paris, 1911.

Edmondston, J., A complete body of Heraldry, London, 1780.

Ekdahl, Sven, Die "Banderia Prutenorum", Göttingen 1976.

Elvin, Charles Norton, A dictionary of Heraldry, East Dereham 1889 & Heraldry Today, London, 1969.

Enciclopedia Italiana (Treccani), III, Araldica, Milano-Roma, 1929.

Enciclopedia universal illustrada Europeo-Americana, vol. 27, Heraldica, Barcelona, 1925.

Encyclopedia Britannica, The, XIII, Heraldry (O. Baron).

Encyclopedia, The catholic, VII, Heraldry (A. C. Fox-Davies, New York, 1910.

Ermens, J., Législation nobiliaire, Bruges, 1780.

Ewald, Wilhelm, Siegelkunde, München, 1914.

Fairbairns, London 1906, Episcopal arms of England & Wales.

Féret, O. P., Fr. H.-M., Les armoiries ou blason de l'Ordre des Frères Prêcheurs dans Archives d'Histoire Dominicaine I, Paris, 1946.

Fesch, Sebastianus, Dissertatio de insigniis erorumque iure, Basileae, 1672.

Fourez, Lucien, Avocat, Le droit héaldique dans les Pays-Bas catholiques, Bruxelles, 1932.

Fox-Davies, Arthur Charles,
a) Fairbairn's book of crests, Edinburgh, 1892.
b) The art of heraldry, London, 1904.
c) Heraldic badges, London, 1906.

d) Heraldry explaines, London, 1907.

e) A complete guide to heraldry, London, 1909; revised by J. P. Brooke-Little, 1969.

Franklyn, Julian, Shield and crest, London, 1960.

Franklyn, Julian and Tanner, John : An Encyclopedic Dictionary of Heraldry. London, 1968.

Freier, Walter, Wappenkunde und Wappenrecht, Leipzig, 1924.

Fretz, Diethelm, Die Zürcher Geistlichkeit bekämpft Kirchenstuhlwappen als verwerfliches Scheinwerk, Separatdruck aus Zwingliana, Bd. VI, Heft 3, SS. 173-188, Zurich, 1935.

Galbreath D(onald) L(indsay),

a) Sigilla Agaunensia, Lausanne, 1927.

b) Sceaux des évêques de Lausanne de 1115-1536, Archives héraldiques suisses, 1929.

c) A treatise on ecclesiastical heraldry, Part I, Papal heraldry, Cambridge, 1930, re-edited by Geoffrey Briggs, Heraldry Today, London, 1972.

d) Handbüchlein der Heraldik, Lausanne, 1930.

e) Manuel du blason, Lausanne et Lyon, 1942 et 1948.

Cf. *Berchem.*

Galbreath, Donald L., & *Vevey*, Hubert de, Manuel d'héraldique, première initiation à l'art et la science du blason, Lausanne, 1922.

Galbreath, D. L. & *Jéquier*, Léon, Lehrbuch der Heraldik, München 1978.

Gardel, Luis D., Les armoiries ecclésistiques au Brésil, Rio de Janeiro, 1963.

Gatterer, Johann Christoph, Wappenkunde, Nürnberg, 1766.

Gavard, Adrien, Les armoiries du diocèse et des évêques de Genève, Extrait des Archives héraldiques suisses, Zurich, 1915.

Gayre, Robert,

a) The heraldry of the Knights of St John Allahabad (India) 1956.

b) The nature of arms, London, 1961.

c) Heraldic cadency, London.

Gérard, B., Histoire de la législation nobiliaire en Belgique, Bruxelles, 1847.

Gerola, Giuseppe, A proposito della iconografia di Innocenzo IV e lo stemma pontificio, Roma, 1931.

Gessler, Ed. A., Bildliche Darstellung der ritterlichen Bewaffnung zur Zeit der Schlacht bei Sempach 1386, Zurich, 1914.

Gevaert, Emile, L'héraldique, son esprit, son langage et ses applications, Bruxelles et Paris (1923).

Gibbon, John, Blason, 1682, re-print in facsimile, Canterbury, 1963.

Giurisprudenza Nobiliare, Ordinamento dello stato nobiliare (1943), Regolamento per la consulta araldica del Regno (1943), Vocabolario araldico, Roma, Rivista Araldica, 1944, 86-144.

Gorino, Mario, Titoli nobiliari e ordini equestri ponticifi, contributo al nuovo diritto araldico concordatario, Torino, 1933.

Grandmaison, Charles M., Dictionnaire héraldique contenant l'explication et la description des termes et figures usités dans le blason, Paris, 1861.

Grant, F. J., The manual of heraldry, Edinburgh, 1924.

Greenwell, Rev. William, und *Blair*, C. H. Hunter, Catalogue of the seals in the treasury of the sea and chapter of Durham, Newcastle, I, 1911; II, 1921.

Gritzner, Adolf Maximilian Ferdinand Grundsätze der Wappenkunst verbunden mit einem Handbuch der heraldischen Terminologie, Nürnberg, 1889.

Gritzner, Erich, Sphragistik, Heraldik, deutsche Munzgeschichte, Berlin, 1912.

Gründel, Paul, Die Wappensymbolik, Leipzig, 1907.

Guigard, Joannis, Bibliothèque héraldique de la France, Paris, 1861.

Armorial du bibliophile, Paris, 1870-72.

Nouvel armorial du Bibliophile, Paris, 1890, I-II.

Guelfi Camajani, Conte G., Dizionario araldico, Milano, 1921.

Guillim, John, A display of heraldry, 6th Edition, London, 1724.

Harot, Eugène.

a) Armorial des évêques et archevêques de Toulouse, Toulouse, 1907.

b) Armorial des évêques de Rieux, Toulouse, 1908.

c) Armorial des évêques de Commings, Toulouse, 1909.

d) Armorial des évêques de la Rochelle, Rome, 1912.

Hauptmann, Felix,

a) Das Wappenrecht, historische und dogmatische Darstellung der im Wappenwesen geltenden Rechtssätze, ein Beitrag zum deutschen Privatrecht, Bonn, 1896.

b) Die Wappen in der Historia Minor des Matthaeus Parisiensis, Jahrb. d. k. k. Gesellschaft "Adler", XIX, neue Serie, II, Wien, 1909.

c) Wappenkunde München und Berlin, 1914.[8]

d) Das Dominikanerwappen, Anal. Ord. Prae-

168

dictatorum, 33 (1925) 224 bis 232, Roma, 1925.
e) Otto Hupp, Wappenkunst und Wappenkunde, Berlin, 1928.
f) Die Papstwappen, Separatdruck aus Zeitschrift für schweiz. Kirchengeschichte, 26. Jahrg., Stans, 1932.

Hefner, O. T. von.
a) Handbuch der theoretischen & praktischen Heraldik, München 1861, 1863.
b) Heraldisches Musterbuch, München, 1862.
c) Altbayrische Heraldik, München, 1869.

Herder, Der Grosse, Bd. 12, Rahmenartikel: Wappen, Freiburg i.B., 1935.

Hildebrandt, Adolf Matthias,
a) Heraldisches Alphabeth, Frankfurt a.M., 1884.
b) Wappenfibel, Frankfurt, a. M. 1893. Görlitz, 1937.
c) Heraldisches Musterbuch für Edelleute, Kunstfreunde, Architekten, Bildhauer, Holzschneider, Graveure, Lithographen, Wappenmaler, Berlin, 1897[3].
d) Heraldik, Neustadt/Aisch, 1970.

Hildebrandt, A. M. & *Seyler*, G. A., Wappenbuch der Ersten, Berlin, 1893.

Hope, H. W., A Grammer of English Heraldry, Cambridge, 1913.

Humphery-Smith, Cecil R.,
a) Heraldry in School Manuals of the Middle Ages, in "The Coat of Arms", July, 1960.
b) General Armory Two, London, 1973.

Hupp, Otto, Münchener Kalender 1893-1935.

Hussmann, Heinrich, Ueber Deutsche Wappenkunst, Wiesbaden, 1973.

Innes of Learney, T., Scots Heraldry, Edinburgh, 1934 & 1956.

Jones, Evan John, Medieval Heraldry, Cardiff, 1943.

Kälde, Bengt Olof,
a) Birgittinsk Ordensheraldik, Heraldisk Tidskrift. Marts 1974. (Copenhagen)
b) Den Svenska Kyrkans heraldik, Heraldisk Tidskrift, Marts 1977. (Copenhagen)

Kephart, Calvin, Origin of armorial insignia in Europe, New York, 1939.

Kirchberger, Johannes, Die Wappen der religiösen Orden, Wien, 1895.

Larusson & Kristjanuson, Sigilla Islandica, Reykjavik I, 1965, II, 1967.

Leigh, Gerard, The accedens of armories, London, 1562.

Le Juge de Segrais, René, Resumo da Ciência do Brasao, Lisboa, 1951.

Leonhard, Walter, Das grosse Buch der Wappenkunst, München, 1976.

Lexikon für Theologie und Kirche, Freiburg i. Br. 1932, Heraldik vol. IV. (Henggeler) & 1960, vol. 5 (Heim).

Lindgren, Uno, Heraldik i svenska författningar, Lund, 1951.

Lynch-Robinson, Sir Christopher, Intelligible Heraldry, London, 1948.

Mackinson of Dunakin, C. R.,
a) Scotlands Heraldry, London, 1948.
b) The Observer's book of Heraldry, London & New York, 1966.

McClatchie, Th. R. H., Japanese Heraldry, Yokohama, 1876.

Mathieu, Remi, Le système héraldique français, Paris, 1946.

Matthieu de Paris, cf. Hauptmann (b).

Mayer, L. A., Saracenic Heraldry, Oxford, 1933.

Menestrier, François-Claude, S. J.,
a) Le véritable art du blason, Lyon, 1659.
b) Abrégé historique des principes héraldiques, Lyon, 1661.
c) Le véritable art du blason et l'origine des armoiries depuis leur institution, Lyon, 1671.
d) Les recherches du blason, Seconde partie, De l'usage des armoiries, Paris, 1673.
e) Le véritable art du blason et l'origine des armoiries, Lyon, 1676.
f) Origine des ornements des armoiries, Paris, 1680.
g) La méthode du blason, Lyon, 1689.
h) La science de la noblesse ou la nouvelle méthode du blason, Paris, 1691.
i) La nouvelle méthode raisonnée du blason, Lyon, 1696 et 1723.

Merz, Walter und *Hegi*, Friedrich, Die Wappenrolle von Zürich, Zürich, 1930.

Meyer-Marthaler, Elisabeth, Die Siegal der Bischöfe von Chur im Mittelalter, Schweiz. Archiv für Heraldik 1944, 1-3 und 54-59, mit VII Tafeln.

Meurgey Jaques, Armorial de l'église de France, évêchés, chapitres, paroisses, abbayes, prieurés, couvents, corporations et communautés religieuses, Macon, 1938.

Mitis, Dr. Oskar Freiherr von, Zur Geschichte der Rangkronen.

Moncreiffe, Iain & Don Pottinger, Simple heraldry cheerfully illustrated, Edinburgh, 1953, reprinted many times.

Moule's Bibliotheca heraldica, London, 1821.

Mure, Kondrad von, Clipearium teutonicum, ca. 1245, ed. by Theodor von Liebenau, Vierteljahrschrift f. Wappen, Siegel & Familienkunde, Jahrg. 17, p. 174 ff., Berlin, 1899.

Naumann, Hans, Die Minnesänger in Bildern der Manessischen Handscrift, Leipzig (1933).

Netzhammer, Raymund, Erzbischof, Stadtwappen auf Münzen pontischer Städte. Vortrag beim VIII. internat. Kongress für Geschichtswissenschaft, gehalten in Zürich am 29. August 1938, Zug, 1938.

Neubecker, Otfried,
  a) Sovietheraldik, in "Osteuropa", Zeitschrift für die gesamten Fragen des europäischen Ostens, 5. Jahrg., Heft 6, 383-392, Berlin, 1930.
  b) Ordensritterliche Heraldik, 1940.
  c) Heraldry, Sources, Symbols and Meaning, London, 1977.

Nisot, Pierre, Le droit des armoiries, Bruxelles, 1924.

Noirot, Marcel, Les armoiries de Sa Sainteté Pie XII, Paris, 1939.

Officer of Arms, An; The Episcopal Arms of England and Wales. London, 1906.

Ordinamento dello stato nobiliare italiano, cf. giurisprudenza nobiliare.

Palliot, Pierre, La vraye et parfaite science des armoiries, Paris, 1664, réimpression fac-similé 1895:

Paradisi, Agostino, Ateneo dell'uomo nobile, Venezia, 1704-1731, I-V.

Pasini Frassoni, Conte Ferruccio,
  a) Araldica italiana, estratto dall'Avvenire no. 29, 20 Aprile 1898, Roma, 1898.
  b) Essai d'armorial des Papes, Collegio Araldico, Roma, 1906.
  c) I cappelli prelatizi, Collegio Araldico, Roma, 1908.

Petrasancta, Silvester, S. J.,
  a) De symbolis heroicis, Romae, 1634.
  b) Tesserae gentilitiae ex legibus fecalibus descriptae, Romae, 1638.

Piferrer, Francisco, Tratado de heraldica y blason, Madrid, 1854. Diccionario de la ciencia heraldica, Madrid, 1861.

Pinches, Rosemary & Anthony Wood, A european armorial, London, 1971, Heraldry Today.

Pinches, J. H. & R. E., The royal heraldry of England, London, 1974, Heraldry Today.

Pine, Leslie G.,
  a) The story of heraldry, London, 1952.

  b) Heraldry & genealogy, London, 1957, 5th edn 1975.
  c) Heraldry, Ancestry & Titles, London, 1965.
  d) International heraldry, London, 1970.

Planché, J. R., The Pursuivant of arms, London, 1873.

Porny, M. A., The elements of heraldry, London, 1795.

Prinet, Max,
  a) L'origine du type des sceaux à l'écu timbré, extrait du Bulletin archéologique, Paris, 1910.
  b) Les insignes des dignités ecclésiastiques dans le blason français du xve siècle, Paris, 1911.
  c) Les characteristiques des Saints dans les armoiries familales, Paris, 1911.
  d) Armoiries combinées d'évêchés et français, Paris, 1911.
  e) L'origine orientale des armoiries européennes, extrait des Archives héraldiques suisses 1912.

Rabino di Borgomale, H.-L., Armorial des évêques de Vence, Nice, 1941.

Raneke & Bökwall, Skandinavisk vapenrulla, Malmö, since 1963.

Raneke, Jan, Bergshammar vapenboken, Lund, 1975.

Rietstap, J. B., Armorial général, Gouda 1884-87, Supplément par V. H. Rolland, La Haye, 1926-34.

Robson, Th., The british Heraldry, Sunderland, 1830.

Rosergio, Bernardus de (Bernard du Rosier), Liber armorum, Paris, Bibl. Nat. lat. 6020, fol 13-44.

Sacken, Eduard Freiherr von, Heraldik, Grundzüge der Wappenkunde, re-edited by Egon Freiherr von Berchem, Leipzig, 1920.

Saint Saud, (Arlot) Comte de,
  a) Blasons, sceaux et devises des archevêques et évêques français de 1906, Vannes, 1906.
  b) Armorial des prélats français, du xixe siècle, Paris, 1906.
  c) Armorial des prélats français du xixe siècle, additions, corrections, détails sigillographiques, Paris, 1908.

Scheffer, C. G. U.,
  a) Heraldik spegel, Stockholm 1964.
  b) Svensk vapenbok för landskap och städer, Stockholm 1967.

Schlegel-Klingspor, Svensk heraldik, Upsala, 1974.

Scohier, Jean, L'état et comportement des armes, Bruxelles 1629.

Seyler, Gustav A., Geschichte der Siegel, Leipzig, 1894. Geschichte der Heraldik, Nürmnerg, 1885.

Smith, Whitney,

a) Flags through the ages & across the world, Maidenhead, 1975.
b) The flag book of the United States, New York, 1975.

Siebmacher's, Johann, Wappenbuch, Faksimile Nachdruck, München, 1975.

Spener, Philippus Jacobus,
a) Theatrum nobilitatis Europeae, Francofurti, 1668.
b) Historia insignium illustrorum, I-IV, Giessae, 1717.
c) Insignium theoria, Francofurti, 1690.

Stalins, (Baron) Gaston,
a) Vovabulaire-Atlas Héraldique en six langues, Paris, 1952.
b) Histoire . . . des Stalins de Flandre et . . . considérations sur le briquet héraldique 2 vols. 1939 & 1945.

Ströhl, H. G.,
a) Heraldischer Atlas, Stuttgart, 1899.
b) Nihon Moncho, Japanisches Wappenbuch, Stuttgart, 1906.
c) Japanische Familienzeichen, "Deutscher Herold", Berlin, 1908.
d) Wappenrolle der Päpste, Album Pontificale, M.-Gladbach, 1909.
e) Heraldik der katholischen Kirche, Berlin, 1910.
f) Die Würdezeichen der katholischen Geistlichkeit, in 'Deutscher Buch- und Steindrucker", XVII, 1053-58, Berlin, 1911.

Sturdza-Saucesti, (Prince) Marcel, Heraldica, Bucuresti, 1974.

Tanner, John : see Franklyn.

T(ausin), H(enri), Armorial des cardinaux, archevêques évêques contemporains de France, Paris, 1874 et 1886.

Tausin, Henri, Dictionnaire des devises ecclésiastiques, Paris, 1907.

Trevor, John, Tractatus Magistri Johannis de Bado Aureo cum Francisco de Foveis de distinctionibus armorum, Brit. Mus. Add. M. S. 29901, XIVth century.

Upton, Nicolas, De studio militari, London, 1496.

Volborth, C. A. von,
a) Wappenrolle der Johanniter in USA & Canada, Cincinnati, 1966.
b) Heraldry in the World. London, 1973.
c) Das Wappen – Stil & Form, Limburg, 1978.
d) Little Manual of Heraldry, Torrance, California, 1966.

Vulson de la Colombière, Marc,
a) La science héroïque, Paris, 1644.

b) De l'office des roys d'armes, des hérauds et des poursuivants, Paris, 1645.

Wagner, Sir Anthony, Garter King of Arms,
a) Catalogue of Heralds, 1934. [Commemorative Exhibition 1934.]
b) Historic Heraldry of Britain, 1939 & 1972.
c) Heralds & Heraldry in the Middle Ages, London, 1939.
d) Heraldry in England, London, 1946, 1949, 1951, 1953.
f) Catalogue of English Mediaeval Rolls of Arms, 1950.
g) The Records & Collections of the College of Arms, London, 1952.
h) English Genealogy, London, 1960.
i) English Ancestry, London, 1961.
k) Heralds of England, London, 1967.
l) Heralds of England, 1967.
m) Aspilogia, London, 1967.
n) Pedigree and Progress, London, 1975.

Warren, A. H., Arms of the Episcopate of Great Britain and Ireland. London 1868.

D. Liturgy, History, Diplomatic

Alcuinus, De divinis officiis, P. L. 101, 1238 ss.

Bernardus, S., Abbas Clarae-Vallensis, Tractatus de moribus et officio Episcoporum, P. L. 182, 809 ss.

Bertini Frassoni, Conte Carlo Augusto, Il Sovrano Militare Ordine di S. Giovanni di Gerusalemme detto di Malta, Roma, 1929.

Boüard, A. de, Manuel de diplomatique française et pontificale, Paris, 1929.

Braun, Joseph, S. J.,
a) Die pontificalen Gewänder des Abendlandes nach ihrer geschichtlichen Entwicklung, Freiburg i. Br. 1898.
b) Die liturgische Gewandung im Okzident und Orient nach Ursprung und Entwicklung, Verwendung und Symbolik, Freiburg i. Br. 1907.

Breslau, Harry, Handbuch der Urkundenlehre für Deutschland und Italien, Berlin-Leipzig, 1931², I-II.

Briquet, Charles Moise, Les filigranes, Dictionnaire historique des marques du papier dès leur apparition vers 1282 jusqu'en 1600, Paris-Genève, 1907, I-IV.

Charon, P. Cyrille (Cyrille Karalevsky), Histoire des Patriarcats Melkites, T. III. Rome et Paris, 1911.

Ciacconius, Alphonsus, O. P. (Oldoni Augustinus, S. J.), Vitae et res gestae Pontificum Romanorum et S. R. E. Cardinalium, Romae, 1677, I-IV.

Denifle, Heinrich, O. P., und *Ehrle*, Franz, S. J., Archiv für Literatur und Kirchengeschichte des Mittelalters, Berlin, 1885-1900, I-VII.

Ehrle, Franz, S. J., Der konstantinische Schatz, cf. Deniflé und Ehrle, Archiv L. K. M., IV.

Fournier, Louis, Soeurs d'Irelande et de Grande Bretagne, Lyon.

Giry, A., Manuel de diplomatique, Paris, 1894 et 1925.

Guarnacci, Mario, Vitae et res gestae Romanorum Pontificum et S. R. E. Cardinalium, Romae, 1751, I-II.

Haine, Abbé Antoine-Joseph-Jacques-François, De la Cour Romaine sous le pontificat de N. S. le pape Pie IX, Louvain, 1859.

Hefele, Prof. Dr. theol. Carl Joseph, Beiträge zur Kirchengeschichte, Archäologie und Liturgik, München, 1863.

Heinecke (Heineccius), Johannes Michael, De veteribus Germanorum aliarumque nationum sigillis, Francofurti et Lipsiae, 1709.

Hontheim, Johannes Nicolaus (von), Historia Trevirensis diplomatica et pragmatica, Augsburg, 1750.

Hugo de Sancto Victore, Speculum Ecclesiae, PL 177, 355 ss.

Isidor de Séville, De ecclesiasticis officiis, PL 83, 739 ss.

Jaffe, Philippus, Res gestae Pontificum Romanorum Lipsiae 1885-88 1, I-II.

Janin, Raymond, Les Églises orientals et les Rites orientaux, troisième édition, Paris, Bonne Presse, 1935.

Kaigorodv, Nestor, Polotsk et ses antiquités historiques et ecclésiastiques, dans la revue "Svetilnik" 1914 n° 2, p. 35, Moscou, février 1914.

Mabillon, Joannes, O. S. B., De re diplomatica, Paris, 1709.

Mann, Mgr H(orace) K., D. D., Tombs and portraits of the popes of the Middle Ages, London, 1929. The lives of the popes of the Middle Ages, London, 1929, I-XV.

Moroni Romano, Gaetano, Dizionario di erudizione storico-ecclesiastica, Venezia, 1840-79, I-CIII, I-VI.

Paoli, Cesare, Diplomatica, nuova edizione aggiornata da G. C. Bascapé, Firenze, 1942.

Persichetti Ugolini di Castel Colbuccaro, Marchese Dott. Eduardo, L'ordine del Santo Sepolcro, Roma, 1931.

Pothast, Augustus, Regesta Pontificum Romanorum, Berlin, 1875.

Richental, Ulrich von, Concilium zu Constanz, Augsburg 1483 édition Fac-simile, Potsdam, 1922.

Serafini, Camillo, Le monete e le bolle plumbee del medagliere Vaticano, Milano 1910-1913, I-II.

Siccardus Cremonensis, Mitrale seu de officiis ecclesiasticis, P. L. 213.

Sickel, Theodor (Ritter von), Beiträge zur Diplomatik, Wien, 1861-82, I-VIII.

Stumpf, Johann, Beschreibung des grossen gemeinen Conciliums zu Constenz, Frankfurt, 1575.

Ughelli, Ferdinando, Italia Sacra sive de Episcopis Italiae, Venetiis, 1717[2].

Zöpfel, F., Urkundenwesen L. Th. K., X, 444 ff., Freiburg i. Br. 1938.

The author wishes to thank Mr. Colin Smythe for preparing the Index and for twelve photographs he took of coats of arms in the author's Liber Amicorum.

INDEX